Mysteries of Isis and Ra

HIEROGLYPHIC TRANSLATION AND PHILOSOPHICAL STUDY OF THE ANCIENT EGYPTIAN SCRIPTURE OF THE MYTH OF ASET AND RA

TRANSLATION BY SEBAI DR. MUATA ASHBY
©2007-2017
Sema Institute
Temple of Aset Shetaut Neter
Kemet University

Mysteries of Isis and Ra

Cruzian Mystic Books
P.O. Box 570459
Miami, Florida, 33257
(305) 378-5432 Fax: (305) 378-6253

First U.S. edition 2017

Copyright 2017 by Reginald Muata Ashby

All rights reserved. No part of this book may be used or reproduced in any manner whatsoever without written permission (address above) except in the case of brief quotations embodied in critical articles and reviews. All inquiries may be addressed to the address above.

The author is available for group lectures and individual counseling. For further information contact the publisher.

Ashby, Reginald Muata
Hieroglyphic Translation of the Ancient Egyptian Myth of Aset and Ra Papyrus ISBN: 1-884564-89-5

Library of Congress Cataloging in Publication Data

1- Ancient Egyptian Religion, 2- Ancient Egyptian Gods and Goddesses, 3- African Religion, 4- African Philosophy.

Sema Institute of Yoga
Cruzian Mystic Books and Music

Mysteries of Isis and Ra
TABLE OF CONTENTS

Contents

- CONTENTS OF THE SCRIPTURE OF THE MYTH OF ASET AND RA: SECTION GUIDE 4
- TABLE OF FIGURES 6
- THE TEACHING COURSE AT KEMETUNIVERSITY.COM: 7
- FOREWORD TO THE NEW TRANSLATION 8
  - EXTENDED TRANSLATION: 8
- PHOTOS OF THE ORIGINAL TEXT: 12
- TRANSLATED SELECTED TEXTS OF THE PERMHERU 16
  - TRANSLATION FORMATS USED FOR PRESENTING THE TRANSLATIONS 16
    - Conventional Interlinear Format 16
    - Trilinear Contextual Format 16
    - Reading the Philosophy Embedded in Ancient Egyptian Hieroglyphic Writings 18
    - Simple determinatives that appear most frequently. 20
- MYTH OF ASET AND RA 26
  - COMPENDIUM OF THE MYTH 27
  - Chapter 7/151 Section 3 Pert-m-Heru Hymn by Aset from PertemHeru- Translation by Dr. Muata Ashby (C) 2000-2013 Sema Institute 30
- SCRIPTURE OF THE MYTH OF ASET AND RA 34
  - SECTION 3: [Verse 12] ASET'S EARLY REFLECTIONS, MEDITATIONS AND CONCLUSIONS 41
- GLOSS ON THE VERSES: Dramatic Reading and Mystic Interpretation of Selected Verses of the Scripture of Aset and Ra 83
  - Transcript of the presentation of the Selected Verses of the Scripture of Aset and Ra at the 2015 Neterian Conference 83
  - Questions and Answers 124
- THE DEEPER MEANING OF THE MYTHS OF THE GODDESS ASET-A GLOSS ON THE MYTH OF RA AND ASET 129
- INDEX 139
- Other Books From C M Books 142

CONTENTS OF THE SCRIPTURE OF THE MYTH OF ASET AND RA: SECTION GUIDE

SECTION: 1- [VERSE 1] SHEDY OF WISDOM AND ASET MEDITATION-LISTENING TO THE TEAACHING PART 1- CREATION AND THE CREATOR --------35

SECTION: 2- [VERSE 7] LISTENING TO THE TEACHING PART 2-UNDERSTANDING THE TROUBLE OF LIFE, DISPASSION, DETACHMENT & CHOICE OF LIFE PATH--------37

SECTION: 3-STUDY ON THE NATURE OF RA (CREATION) --------42

SECTION: 4 - [VERSE 18] SHEDY OF ACTION & DEVOTION (EMOTION) TO GOD IN FORM OF RA-TEM; A RITUAL OBSERVANCE IN LATE AFTERNOON, DEVOTIONAL REMEMBRANCE & MEDITATION, VIEWING RA AND COLLECTING RA'S LIFE FORCE EMANATIONS TO BUILD CONCENTRATION ON RA & SPIRITUAL STRENGTH FOR ONE-POINTEDNESS OF MIND ON THE FORMS, MOVMENTS AND ACTIONS OF RA--------44

SECTION: 5 – [VERSE 19] SHEDY OF ACTION AND RIGHT RITUAL- DISCIPLINE OF WORKING DAY BY DAY – GATHERING SPIRITUAL STRENGTH AND STAMINA =FASHIONING ONESELF INTO THE SACRED SERPENT FOR ONE-POINTED VISION --------45

SECTION: 6- [VERSE 22] SHEDY OF MEDITATION (CONCENTRATION)-DISCIPLINE OF FOCUS ON RA, THOUGHTS DIRECTED AT THE DIVINE, PATIENCE AND STRIKING AT THE RIGHT TIME --------47

SECTION: 7- [VERSE 30] SHEDY OF ASET MEDITATION (WITNESSING & REFLECTING)-DISCIPLINE OF BEHOLDING THE FLUTTER OF CREATION CONFIRMING ITS ILLUSORINESS AS RA & GODS AND GODDESSES FALTER IN MAINTAINING HIS LIFE WHICH SUSTAINS CREATION AFTER BEING BITTEN BY THE SACRED SERPENT--------49

SECTION: 8- [VERSE 47] SHEDY OF WISDOM (SEBAIT-PHILOSOPHY)-DISCIPLINE OF UNDERSTANDING THERE IS A SECRET NATURE OF GOD (RA) THAT WAS HITHERTO UNKNOWN AND NEEDS TO BE DISCOVERED IN ORDER TO ATTAIN THE GOAL OF LIFE --------55

SECTION: 9-SUMMARY 54-61: RA EXPLAINS HIS ILLNESS AND CALLS FOR THE GODS AND GODDESSES WHO ARE SKILLFUL IN HEALING WORDS OF POWER TO COME TO HIM FROM ALL OVER CREATION. --------58

SECTION: 10- [VERSE 62] SHEDY OF WISDOM-UNDERSTANDING RA AND THE COSMIC FORCES ARE POWERLESS BEFORE THE MIGHT OF A SERIOUS, DISPASSIONATE, RELENTLESS & REGULAR -NOT INTERMITTENT SPIRITUAL ASPIRANT--------61

SECTION: 11-SUMMARY 71-78: SHEDY OF ACTION AND WISDOM (ANTET BEGAG) NOT BEING DECIEVED BY RA AND HIS ILLUSORY CREATION--------64

SECTION: 12- [VERSE 79] SHEDY OFACTION AND WISDOM AND MEDITATION (LASER FOCUS ON GOAL OF LIFE) ASET UNDETERRED, ASKS RA FOR HIS NAME –WITH SPECIAL WORDS OF POWER-AS A CONDITION OF PROVIDING THE CURE--------67

SECTION: 13-SUMMARY V83-93: SHEDY OF ACTION, MEDITATION, WISDOM-RELENTLESS INSISTANCE, (ANTET BEGAG) AND NOT BEING DISUADED -AFTER BEING ASKED ABOUT HIS NAME RA TRIES TO, IN A FUTILE EFFORT, TO DISUADE ASET BY OFFERING MORE MISINFORMATION ABOUT HIS NATURE AND NAME- CULMINATING IN THE PROCLAMATION OF HIS THREE MAIN FORMS --------69

SECTION: 14- [VERSE 97] SHEDY OF ACTION WISDOM FOCUS AND NON-STOP (RELENTLESS) INSISTANCE (AN CHEN) -WITHOUT STOPPING HER EFFORTS--------74

SECTION: 15- [VERSE 102] RA RELENTS AND AGREES TO OPEN HIMSELF UP FOR ASET TO ENTER HIM AND DISCOVER HIS REAL NAME-HERE ENDS THE LOWER MEDITATION PRACTICE AND THE GOAL OF THE SACRED SERPENT HAS BEEN ACHIEVED-DISARMING RA (CREATION) AND ALLOWING ITS ESSENTIAL NATURE TO BE DISCOVERED BY JOINING WITH IT. SO AT THIS POINT THERE ARE NO MORE THOUGHTS< CHANT OR CONCENTRATION OR FOCUS ON THE IMAGES OF RA--------76

SECTION: 16- VERSES 109-114-RA'S NAME OFFICIALLY DISCOVERED-ASET DECLARES SHE WILL CURE RA AND BANISH THE POISON ALLOWING HIS HEALTH AND VISION --------79

SECTION: 17-[VERSE 114] SHEDY OF NEHAST NEFERHETEP (RESTING IN THE DIVINE ABODE-THRONE OF RA) ASET RESTORES RA TO HEALTH WITH SPECIAL WORDS OF POWER TO HEAL THE MIND AND SOUL HURT BY THE DELUSIONS OF LIFE AND THEREBY ALLOWS CREATION TO REVERT BACK TO ITS ILLUSORY FORM AND RA RETURNS TO CREATING, SUSTAINING, AND CONCLUDING THE DAYS, AND YEARS AS BEFORE --------------------81

SECTION: 18-[VERSE 117] ASET PROVIDES INSTRUCTIONS FOR ANYONE WISHING TO FOLLOW THIS PATH BY A RITUAL THAT INCLUDES: UTTERING THE WORDS OF POWER SHE USED, WITH THE INTENT, FEELING, RELENTLESS INTENSITY SHE APPLIED-ALL TO BE DONE IN FRONG OF SPECIAL IMAGES------------------------------82

TABLE OF FIGURES

FIGURE 1: TEMPLE OF ASET AT PILAK 7
FIGURE 2: TRAINING OF SCRIBES - FIGURE: ANCIENT EGYPTIAN SCHOOL COPY BOOK 9
FIGURE 3: CURSIVE WRITING IN ANCIENT EGYPT 9
FIGURE 4: SECTION OF THE PAPYRUS OF ANI 10
FIGURE 5: HIERATIC SCRIPT SAMPLE FROM THE MIDDLE KINGDOM PERIOD TO THE COPTIC PERIOD (ILLUSTRATION -) 10
FIGURE 6: PHOTOS OF THE ORIGINAL TEXT OF STORY OF ASET AND RA 12
FIGURE 7: PHOTOS OF THE ORIGINAL TEXT OF STORY OF ASET AND RA 2 13
FIGURE 8: PHOTOS OF THE ORIGINAL TEXT OF STORY OF ASET AND RA 3 14
FIGURE 9: PHOTOS OF THE ORIGINAL TEXT OF STORY OF ASET AND RA 4 15
FIGURE 10: SLIDE FROM 2007 NETERIAN CONFERENCE 26
FIGURE 11: COVER FROM BOOK MYSTERIES OF ISIS 27
FIGURE 12: IMAGES OF ASET AND RA FROM HISTORICAL ANCIENT EGYPTIAN ICONOGRAPHY 28
FIGURE 13: IMAGES OF STATUES OF ASET AND RA 29
FIGURE 14: REVIEW-LISTENING REFLECTION AND MEDITATION FROM 2007 NETERIAN CONFERENCE 38
FIGURE 15: ARTIST RENDITION OF IMAGE OF THE BOAT OF RA FROM CONTEMPORARY PAPYRUS 42
FIGURE 16: TEM IN HIS BOAT AND THEN ABSENT 77
FIGURE 17: VERSES 8-10 OF THE ANCIENT EGYPIAN ANUNIAN CREATION SCRIPTURE 84
FIGURE 18: (ON FOLLOWING PAGE) FROM THE BOOK OF COMING FORTH BY DAY-HYMN TO ASAR 87
FIGURE 19: ANCIENT EGYPTIAN IMAGE OF THE THREE FORMS OF RA: RA-KHEPRI (KHEPERA), RA-HERAKHTY AND RA-TEM 97
FIGURE 20: SUNRAYS OF RA SHINE ON THE FOREHEAD OF ASET 99
FIGURE 21: AKHENATON AND NEFERTITI RECEIVING RAYS FROM ATON 100
FIGURE 22: REVIEW-PMH CHAP 30 -HEART AS CAUSE OF INCARNATION 104
FIGURE 23: SOLAR BOAT OF KING KHUFU BUILT OF CEDAR -VIEW 1- REFERRING TO THE SOLAR BOAT OF RA 105
FIGURE 24: SOLAR BOAT OF KING KHUFU VIEW 2 106
FIGURE 25: THE THIRD PHASE OF RA: RA-TEM 107
FIGURE 26: (ON FOLLOWING PAGE) ARTISTIC MODERN CONCEPT ILLUSTRATION OF RA GETTING BITTEN BY ASET'S SERPENT 107
FIGURE 27: TEM IN HIS BOAT AND THEN ABSENT 118
FIGURE 28: TEACHINGS OF TEMPLE OF ASET (ISIS) MEDITATION MAT/POSTER 122

THE TEACHING COURSE AT KEMETUNIVERSITY.COM:

The full translation of the Hieroglyphic Scripture of Aset and Ra was presented with more extensive commentary and details in the Course entitled *Teaching of the Temple of Aset. Original translation ©2015-2016 Dr. Muata Ashby.* The text was presented at the 2016 Neterian Conference in Miami, Florida Dec. 2016

As a matter of context, it is useful to know that one of the places where this scripture would have been studied in ancient times. The center of worship of Aset (Isis) in ancient times was the temple of Aset. There were some main large temple complexes dedicated to Aset but other Aset worship centers have been discovered throughout Egypt and around the ancient world including Greece, Italy and other parts of Europe. One of the main centers of worship in ancient times was the temple of Aset at Pilak or Philae Island in the south of Egypt.

Figure 1: Temple of Aset at Pilak

FOREWORD TO THE NEW TRANSLATION

The following is an extended translation of the same sections of the text that were presented in the 2007 Neterian Conference in Atlanta Ga. Plus the rest of the Hieroglyphic scripture of the Teaching of Aset and Ra. The present volume contains a complete text translation of the entire hieroglyphic scripture known as the Myth of Ra and Aset, currently housed in the Turin Museum in Turin Italy.

EXTENDED TRANSLATION:

This present volume constitutes an extended translation of the text, meaning that the previous translations by Dr. Ashby have not only ben revised but also expanded in such a way as to present more of the background research leading to the translations as well as presenting associated texts that bring greater depth to the study of the present main text. Therefore, this volume will have more notes and references than the previous works which were more designed for PowerPoint presentation media.

The subject of the ancient Egyptian hieratic text was covered in Lesson 1 of the *course entitled Teaching of the Temple of Aset* and in the book *Ancient Egyptian Hieroglyphs for Beginners: Medtu Neter Divine Words* by Dr. Muata Ashby. The following is a brief summary with excerpts from the book containing helpful points for the present study.

> The word "hieroglyph" comes from the Greek terms "*hieros*" (sacred) and "*glypho*" (inscriptions). The term was first used by Clement of Alexandria. In ancient times the classical Greek writer, Plutarch, stated in his rendition of the ancient Egyptian myth of Isis and Osiris that the ancient Egyptian language had 25 consonants.[1]
>
> The earliest known dated forms of hieroglyphic writing in Egypt have been dated by Egyptologists at 3,400 B.C.E. The latest dated inscription in hieroglyphs was made on the gatepost of a temple at Philae in c. 394 A.C.E.[2]
>
> The formal hieroglyphic script was used extensively and mostly for formal inscriptions on the temple walls, coffins, and tombs. In many inscriptions, the hieroglyphs are very painstakingly carved with much detail, in full color. In some uses, they are rendered in simple outlines. For everyday usages and papyrus scriptures, the cursive hieroglyphic or the Hieratic scripts were used.[3]

---

[1] Book Ancient Egyptian Hieroglyphs for Beginners by Dr. Muata Ashby
[2] ibid
[3] ibid

Figure 2: TRAINING OF SCRIBES - Figure: Ancient Egyptian School Copy book

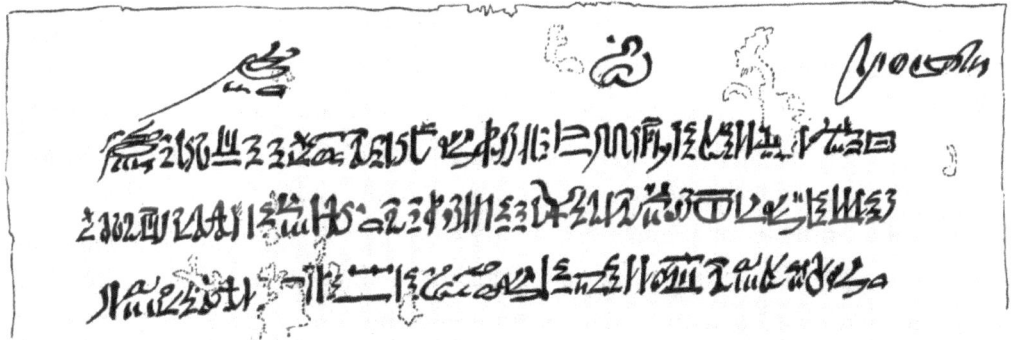

UPPER PART OF A PAGE OUT OF A SCHOOL COPY-BOOK.

The text runs: "Harvest. The worm took half of the food, the hippopotamus the other half. Many mice were in the field, the locusts, the cattle ate; the sparrows stole. Woe (?) to the farmers! The remainder, which is in the threshing floor, the thieves made an end of for him, ..." The word 'aska = much, at the end of the first line, is corrected, as well as the sign te in the middle of the third line, both of which were not written well enough by the otherwise not unskilful scribe. (After An. 5, 16.)

There were elementary schools where the basics of *Medtu Neter* were taught. It was one of the main subjects. Advanced training was given as the scribe worked as an apprentice. Training included laborious copying of texts which were considered "classics" and these included the wisdom text literature such as the teachings of Ptahotep and the Teachings of Ani. Training was first given in cursive hieroglyphic and then in hieratic and then also in formal hieroglyphic. An example of an ancient Egyptian exercise tablet, wherein the scribes were learning the hieratic script, is given above.[4]

Figure 3: CURSIVE WRITING IN ANCIENT EGYPT

The cursive practice of the written language influenced not so much the form of the hieroglyphic but the spellings and grammar of the hieroglyphic. These factors along with the actual penmanship of the scribes are some of the aspects that present substantial difficulty in understanding certain periods of writing. Examples of hieroglyphic are compared with two different periods of hieratic below:[5]

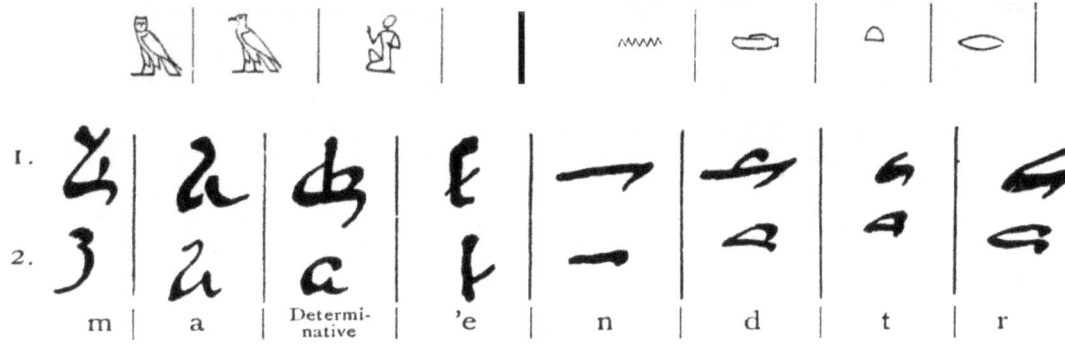

---

[4] ibid
[5] ibid

1- Middle Egyptian (Middle Kingdom), 2- New Egyptian (New Kingdom)

Thus, the different periods of the writing can be correlated, but the styles and spelling forms of different periods make it necessary to specialize in the study of particular periods in order to understand and grasp the particularities of that period. Consequently, Egyptologists who may specialize in a particular period might be able to read most texts from that period, but could not read most texts of other periods without frequently consulting a dictionary for that period's writings, because the words would appear differently from period to period, and there could also be some variation due to the penmanship of the scribe. So the hieroglyphic script did not change in form, but in grammar, but the cursive script had many changes in form and in grammar.[6]

Old Kingdom Cursive Hieroglyphic Script[7] (Also known as Cursive Hieroglyphic- most resembles the Hieroglyphic script)[8]

Figure 4: Section of the Papyrus of Ani

↓

The Middle Kingdom to Late Period Hieratic Script

(Hieratic was a shorthand hieroglyphic script; it was used by the priests and priestesses.)

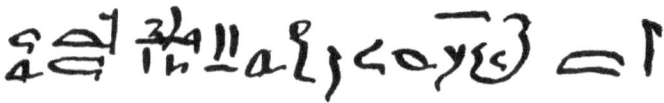

Figure 5: Hieratic script sample from the Middle Kingdom period to the Coptic period (illustration -[Mercer, p. 2]**)**

---

[6] ibid
[7] ibid
[8] Image from *Egyptian Book of the Dead*. E. W. Budge (1899)

Hieratic is an adaptation of the hieroglyphic for ease of use in writing non-monumental texts, especially those that involve extensive expositions of the philosophical teachings and myths on papyrus paper and other literary compositions; it was used since Pre-Dynastic times. This form of the script appears on various papyri known as "Coffin Texts" and "Book of the Dead," i.e., Prt-m-Hru. This script developed into regional variants and period variants from the early period to the late period of ancient Egyptian history.[9]

Hieratic developed in succeeding levels of "cursiveness" from the Middle Kingdom to the Coptic Period. The development of cursive writing included a tendency to reduce the number of glyphs used. Many ancient Egyptian texts are written in hieratic, so Egyptologists transcribe them into hieroglyphic for easier study. [10]

---

[9] ibid
[10] ibid

PHOTOS OF THE ORIGINAL TEXT:

The Following are photos of the original text which uses the hieratic script, now housed at the Turin Museum in Turin, Italy. Photos ©2015 by Dr. Muata Ashby

Figure 6: PHOTOS OF THE ORIGINAL TEXT of Story of Aset and Ra

Figure 7: PHOTOS OF THE ORIGINAL TEXT of Story of Aset and Ra 2

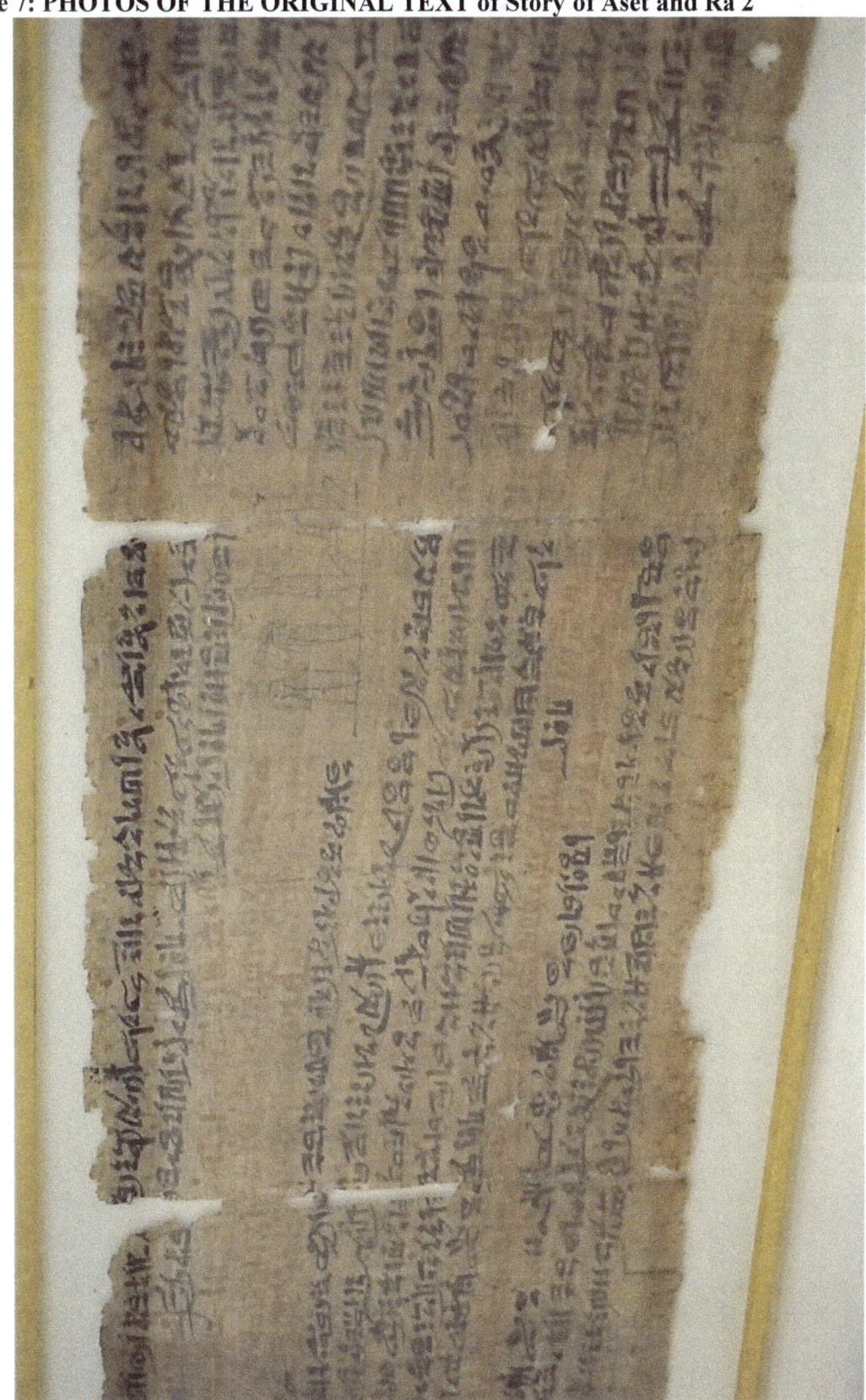

Figure 8: PHOTOS OF THE ORIGINAL TEXT of Story of Aset and Ra 3

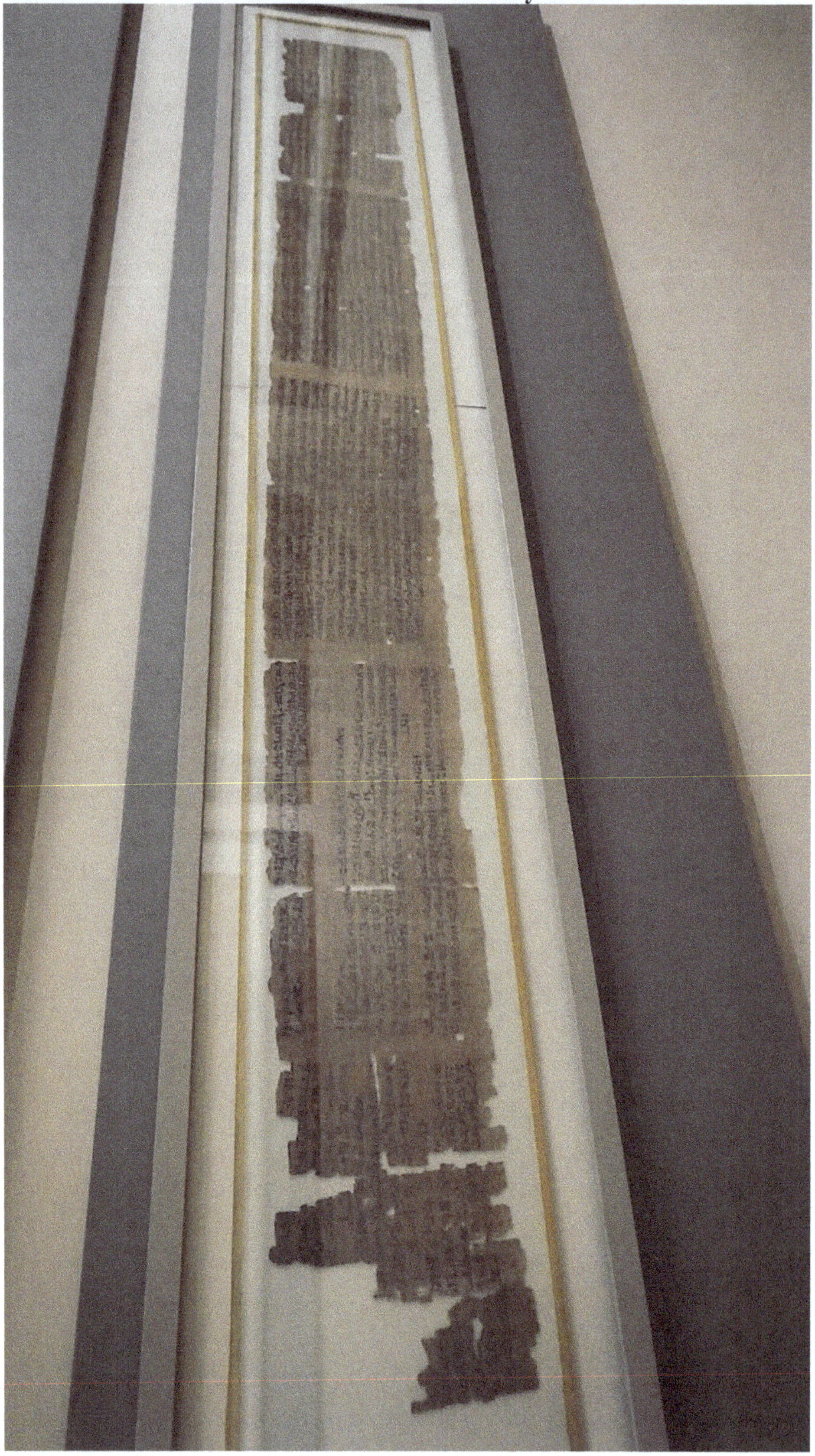

Figure 9: PHOTOS OF THE ORIGINAL TEXT of Story of Aset and Ra 4

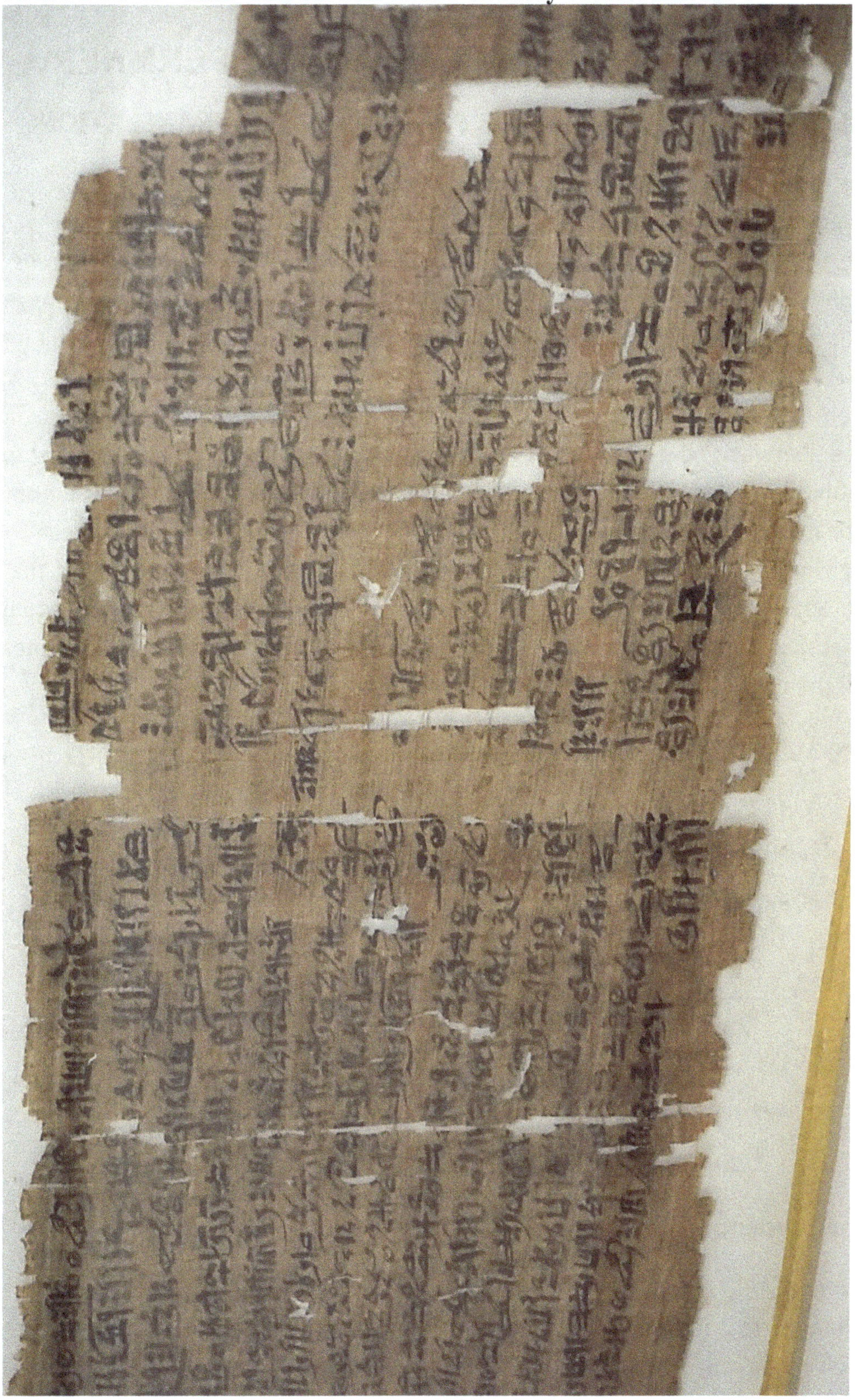

TRANSLATED SELECTED TEXTS OF THE PERMHERU

TRANSLATION FORMATS USED FOR PRESENTING THE TRANSLATIONS

Conventional Interlinear Format

The conventional or regular interlinear format of translating Ancient Egyptian hieroglyphic texts presents a phonetic transliteration of the Ancient Egyptian hieroglyphs and transposes the hieroglyphs into the characters of the language they are being translated into. The second line presents a word for word translation. This level of translation can sometimes result in a limited, choppy and less intelligible presentation of the original intent of the script. When the translation is between languages of dissimilar structure and cultural references such as the difference between the Ancient Egyptian language, which is rich in metaphor and iconographical implied wisdom versus the European languages which are based on a stricter alphabetic matrix, the structural differences along with differences of culture mean that a strict word for word translation can be insufficient to convey a full understanding of the intended meaning. So, while the conventional interlinear format is useful to a certain extent, a more comprehensive translation matrix is needed to gain the deeper richness of the meaning and import of the original hieroglyphic text.

An Example of the Regular Interlinear Format:

Verse 1. ORIGINAL TEXT

    1.1. Transliteration into the phonetic letters of the language of the reader

    1.2. Translation into the words of the language of the reader

Ex:

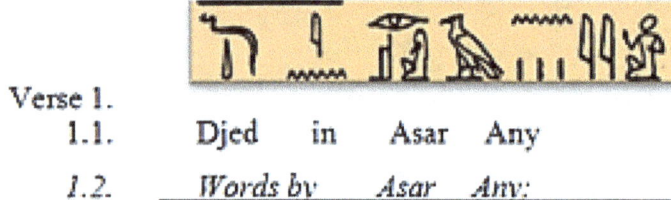

Verse 1.
1.1.   Djed   in   Asar   Any
1.2.   *Words by   Asar   Any:*

Trilinear Contextual Format

The Trilinear Format for translating the Ancient Egyptian writing is a method as well as, to some degree, also a decipherment protocol that allows a layout for viewing the meaning from its source through layers of meaning extraction to the final rendition. The term "decipherment" is used because to the modern mind, whose concerns are often far removed from the world and philosophy of the Ancient Egyptians, the contexts and philosophy of the ancients is akin to more than a mystery, but also as a scarcely fathomable idea that is like a code or formula to be discovered so as to unlock the secrets of life, death, and the afterlife. Over the years, Dr. Muata Ashby has developed a format of translating Ancient Egyptian hieroglyphs into the native language of the reader that incorporates three levels of translation instead of the two levels of the ordinary conventional interlinear format. In a few cases, the conventional interlinear format is used in this volume. However, in most other cases a Ternary System will be used. The Ternary System devised by Dr. Muata Ashby adds a third layer of translation to the work that includes a contextual translation beyond the word for word translation. This added layer of translation may be termed "Contextual Translation" and altogether constitutes the ***Trilinear Contextual format***.

The Trilinear Form (which is a ternary system) of translations is a format developed by Dr. Muata Ashby for translating the Ancient Egyptian Hieroglyphic texts. It contains a *tripartite* arrangement composed of three translation sections or layers/levels. The <u>first level</u> is a phonetic transliteration. The <u>second level</u> is a direct word for word translation from hieroglyphic to the native language of the reader. These two levels generally constitute the "Conventional Interlinear Format" of translation. The Trilinear Format adds a new level of translation. The <u>third level</u> of translation is a contextual translation bringing out the meaning in an informal colloquial context in prose style incorporating: A- the Ancient Egyptian Sebait (philosophical) tenets along with B- the Ancient Egyptian Matnu (mythic) references and Ancient Egyptian "Maut" (morals or takeaways of the myth to which the text appertains) contained in the text in order to better reveal the intended meaning for the reader's language and culture.

An example of the Trilinear Format:

Verse 1.   ORIGINAL TEXT

    1.1. Transliteration into the phonetic letters of the language of the reader

    1.2. Translation into the words of the of the language of the reader

    1.3. Translation with contextual insights which may include philosophical and or

        mythological and/or historical background insights with colloquial references.

Ex:

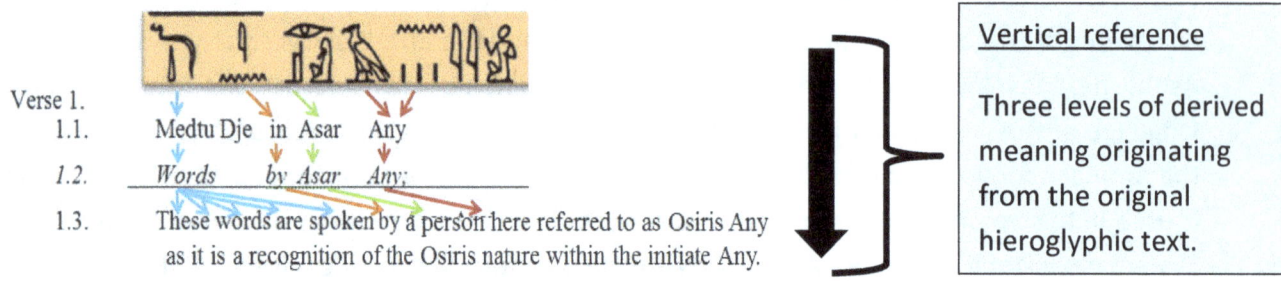

NOTE: Each level of translation is designed to be both a reference to the other levels (vertically) but also to the previous and next statement in each level; so for example Verse translation Level 2.1 relates to 2.2 and 2.3 (vertical) but 2.2 also relates to 1.2 and 3.2 (horizontal). Therefore, if all the Level 2 translations are read by themselves or Level 3 translations are read by themselves one after the other, there will be a continuous and coherent rendering of the text

Example

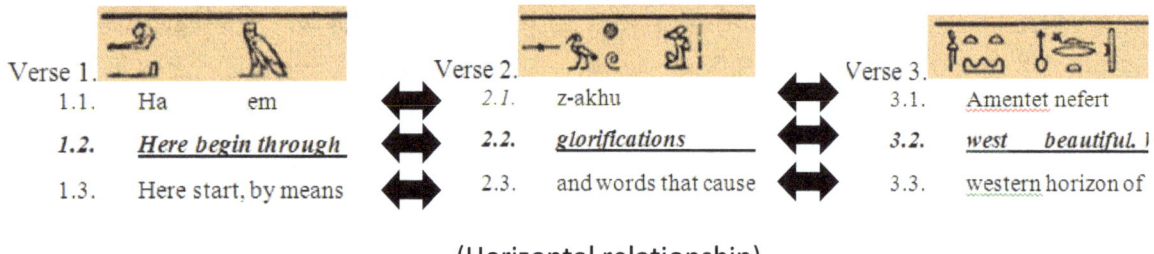

(Horizontal relationship)

In this way, the readings of Verse 1.2 followed by Verse 2.2, followed by Verse 3.2, translations, one after the other (ignoring .1 and .3 levels), horizontally, provide a continuous and coherent word for word narrative of the translation.

Also, the readings of Verse 1.3 followed by Verse 2.3, followed by Verse 3.3, translations, one after the other (ignoring .1 and .2 levels), horizontally, provide a continuous and coherent prose narrative of the translation.

Reading the Philosophy Embedded in Ancient Egyptian Hieroglyphic Writings

Here I will provide two examples, using two of the most important hieroglyphs to demonstrate why and how the philosophy of the Ancient Egyptian Mysteries is determined in the texts to be read. As stated earlier, reading the Ancient Egyptian texts in a literal way, ascribing meanings that relate to the culture of the reader is a disservice to the ancient culture and also it is a distortion of the meaning of the texts and the legacy of the original priests and priestesses who created them.

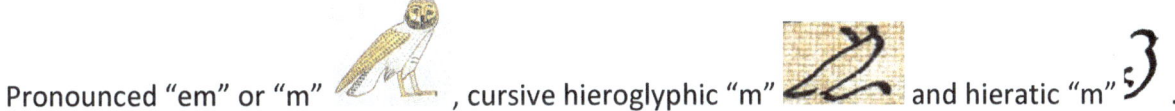

Pronounced "em" or "m", cursive hieroglyphic "m" and hieratic "m".

The first glyph is the owl. Perhaps one of the most important glyphs, unlike determinatives, which do not convey phonetic aspects to the word, the owl has phonetic and philosophical meaning. Whenever the owl appears the meaning can range from "in, within, inside, though, as, in the form of." This means that it is a pivotal term especially when it relates the person for whom the text has been created to any particular or general Divinity [god or goddess]. It, therefore, means that such a person is being identified with that divinity or with an aspect of divinity or they are being recognized as "becoming, or appearing or manifesting as". This, of course, signifies a movement of transformation either in progress or already attained. This glyph is seldom interpreted in such a manner and thus the overall outcomes of such neglectful translations will render a mundane and or erroneous insight into the Ancient Egyptian hieroglyphic writings.

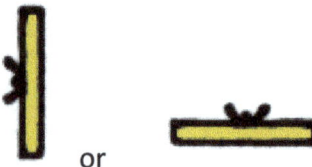

Another important glyph is the scroll.

Generally, the Ancient Egyptian language is composed of phonetic, ideographic and determinative glyphs. The determinative glyphs do not contribute a phonetic aspect to the word but rather contributes a reference and or philosophical implication to be inferred by the reader. The scroll is a determinative glyph that, when appears, forces the application of a perspective abstractness that allows a vision of a meaning that transcends a strictly mundane or specific application. This is a reading that incorporates a philosophical and or conceptual basis to the meaning of the particular word. An example of how to apply the scroll in reading a word or sentence or passage is that its conceptual abstractness is to be applied to the regular meaning of the world, and the abstractness relates to the Ancient Egyptian philosophy of the spiritual mysteries that affirms a transcendental nature of life that goes beyond physical reality.

As a group, determinatives provide a similar function and constitute an integral and essential means of understanding the deeper wisdom and intent of the Ancient Egyptian written language. Below are some of the most important determinatives.

Simple determinatives that appear most frequently.

Determinatives are symbols that convey a general or specific meaning to a word. They are un-vocalized and are only to be read; they are placed at the end of a word, so they also act as word dividers. Very rarely some texts have been found using a small dot to separate units of thought. They occur less frequently in the older texts and more frequently in later texts. Thus, there is an indication that the classical form of the language is not the "original" form but a development of it. The earlier form, as depicted in Pre-Dynastic inscriptions, is more of an ideographic and phonetic (alphabetic) system. Determinatives are an advantage because they determine what type of word is being read, and they also separate words. The use of determinatives becomes more important the more ideograms are used when there are fewer vowels used, and when there is less phonetic complementation in a word. In any case, to revive the language, it would be advantageous to create a standard for the spelling of words. This could be accomplished by spelling out words and using phonetic complements and vowels. Then there would be less need for determinatives. The ancient Egyptian language has within itself the capacity to support a range of options for its usage, as the evidence for these forms can be found in varied texts or in varying periods of ancient Egyptian history. The usage of any of these forms does not affect the orthography (letters and their sequences in words) or syntax (the grammatical arrangement of words in sentences i.e. sentence structure.

Some determinatives can be associated with one word. Others can be associated with a class of words. For example, the seated robed man with long beard 𓀀 lets us know that all the words it appears with are about a God. These kinds of determinatives are referred to by scholars as *Generic Determinatives*. A list of common generic determinatives is below:

✓ Many ancient Egyptian words have the same apparent consonant spelling which is differentiated only by the determinative (as explained earlier, which would not be necessary if there was more use of the vowels). However, the determinative can provide a more precise feeling for the genre of a word and its relation to contexts that go beyond the strictly phonetic values. So there can be many dimensions of meaning depending on the particular choice of the spelling of the word and the particular determinative used.

The word *rek* can have different meanings depending on the determinative used to assign a reference meaning to the word:

Ex. 1: *rek* = time - determinative used ☉ (sundisk)

Ex. 2: *rekh* = burn - determinative used 🔥 (fire)

In the written language, determinatives allow a great range of words to sound alike and yet have different meanings - determined by the determinatives. Of course, this would lead to confusion if the script were to be read out loud unless the context was understood; but some of the written language is designed primarily to be read instead of written. The examples below illustrate this aspect of the "determinization" in ancient Egyptian writing.

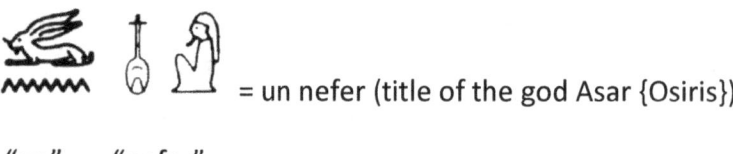 = un nefer (title of the god Asar {Osiris})

"un"   "nefer"

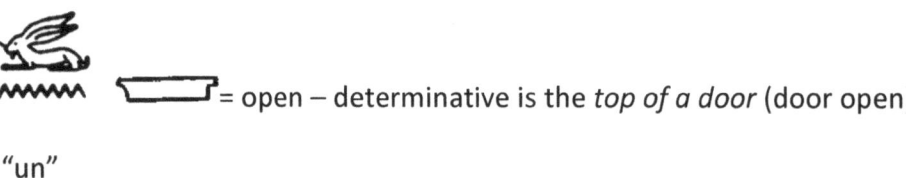 = open – determinative is the *top of a door* (door open)

"un"

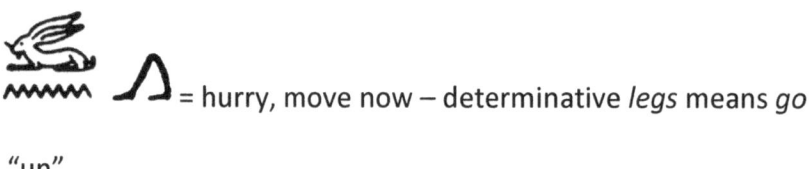 = hurry, move now – determinative *legs* means *go*

"un"

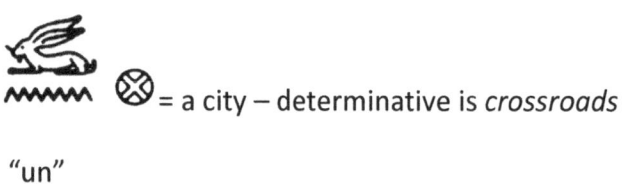 = a city – determinative is *crossroads*

"un"

Important Points

- ✓ Because there are many similar spellings, the language lends itself to a great capacity for punning and poetic literature.
- ✓ Many of the ancient Egyptian words have meanings that do not need to be memorized because the determinative helps the interpretation of the meaning when it is encountered.
- ✓ In the Hieratic script, the scribes tended to use more determinatives than the carved monuments and hieroglyphic inscriptions. However, a modern effort to revive the language could benefit from adopting a set number of determinatives as in order to facilitate the learning and reading process.

1. This is a non-alphabetical symbol called "shenu" used to enclose royal names – it is often referred to as a "cartouche" in modern culture. So, any time you see this you will know that there is a royal name being depicted. It is actually an elongated *shen* symbol. The ⌒*shen* or ⚬ is a rope tied into a circle; the *shen* means "eternity."

2. This symbol represents a man sitting. It signifies the word "I" or "me".

3. This symbol represents a woman sitting. It signifies that the person is female.

4. calling, hail

5. Actions of the mouth, speaking, eating; can also relate to thinking because speech is the pathway of expression for the mind's thoughts.

6. inertness, tired, sloth, listless

7. effort, strength, force – used in the word *nekht* - strong, forceful

8. Actions of the legs, walking, moving towards. When used in the opposite to the direction of the text, it means moving away ∧.

9. This symbol represents a man seated with a beard. It signifies that the person is a god.

Mysteries of Isis and Ra

10. "Arat" – This symbol represents a cobra. It signifies that the person is a "goddess".

11. "Neter" - This symbol represents a "standard." It signifies that the text relates to divinity – can be a god, goddess or androgynous or abstract divinity without gender.

12. Ra (sundisk) this symbol can be used to determine the god Ra and also different words that convey the different aspects of time and the passage of time.

13. fire, hot, burning.

14. animal

15. tree, greenery

16. road, path, way

17. knife, to cut

18. (Sparrow) something small, petty, negative, bad, defective

19. a piece of land

20. "ta" land

21. "ta" land

22. flesh, skin

23. This symbol represents a crossroads. It signifies that the word it appears in is a town.

24. *mdjat* {medjat}- This symbol represents a "scroll," or a "book" and can generally symbolize wisdom as in the

wisdom that is contained in a scroll written by a sage containing wisdom teachings or philosophy. It also means that the meaning of the word it appears in is not exactly the mundane meaning suggested by the words themselves but goes beyond that –so it is an abstract rendition of the mundane meaning.

25. ▱ This symbol represents the "sky" or in some cases "heaven" and is called "pet".

For more on the Ancient Egyptian Hieroglyphic Writing, see the book *Ancient Egyptian Hieroglyphs for Beginners* by Muata Ashby

MYTH OF ASET AND RA

This present volume is not primarily a mythological study of the Myth of Aset and Ra, upon which the text is based. That study has occurred in and was recorded at the 2007 Neterian Conference and was included in Lesson 2 of the *course entitled Teaching of the Temple of Aset*, currently being offered at the Kemet University. Nevertheless, the myth is recounted in the text though that will not be the main focus of this current study. The focus of this current study is the hieroglyphic text itself and the sebait or philosophical teaching contained in it that is within the mythological renderings.

Figure 10: Slide from 2007 Neterian Conference

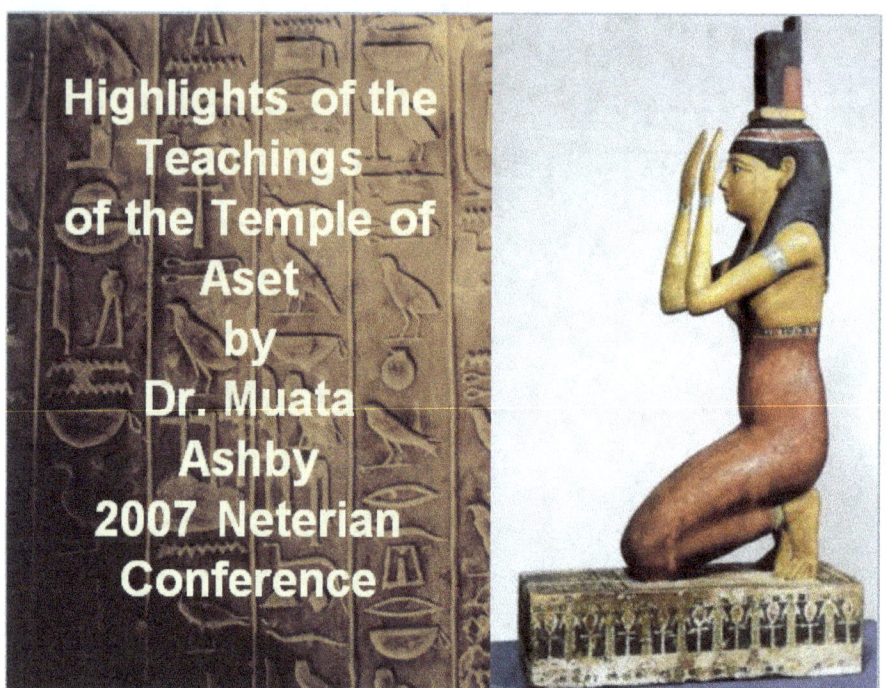

The following summary of the myth is presented as a reminder only. For a more detailed study go to Lesson 2 of the Teachings of the Temple of Aset course at Kemet University or to the 2007 Neterian Conference recordings and proceedings.

COMPENDIUM OF THE MYTH

FROM THE BOOK *MYSTERIES OF ISIS* By Sebai Muata Ashby

Figure 11: Cover from book Mysteries of Isis

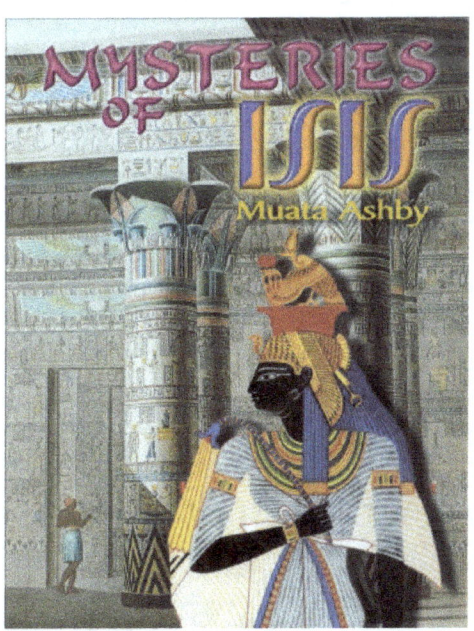

The following summary is a brief introduction to the most important spiritual scripture of the Temple of Aset and was studied by the initiates, priests, and priestesses of her temple. To do so under the guidance of the temple sages is the act of following and remaining close to the Goddess as enjoined by the initiatic practice. This scripture and the detailed study of the hieroglyphic text is the central study in the Teachings of the Temple of Aset course.

COMPENDIUM OF THE MYTH OF RA AND ASET

> This is the story of Ra and Aset. Ra is the Supreme Divinity. Ra is the source of all Creation. Ra is the essence of all life, fire, the gods and goddesses, men and women, beasts, cattle, reptiles, birds, fish and all objects in Creation. Ra's names and forms are innumerable and unknowable even by the gods and goddesses. Ra is so ancient that periods of one hundred and twenty-five years for human beings are like periods of a year for him.

> Behold the goddess Aset. She was living in the form of a woman in ancient times. She was knowledgeable in the words of power and the wisdom of the world. Aset had no desire for human existence. She was dispassionate towards human beings. She revered the state of the gods and goddesses and revered, even more, the state of the spirits, because they were closer to the Divine.

Aset meditated in her heart as follows, "Is it possible for me to become like Ra and to be the supreme monarch of all Creation by knowing the name of Ra?"

One day as Ra made his entrance in the eastern horizon, a portion of his essence fell upon the earth. Aset took this and mixed it with earth and fashioned it into the form of a serpent. She left the serpent on the road which the great god traveled. The serpent bit Ra and caused him to become ill. He became so ill that the gods and goddesses feared he would die. Nobody could find an antidote to the serpent's bite.

Then Aset came along to speak to her father Ra and said: "What is this, Oh Divine Father? What is it? Hath a serpent shot his venom into thee? Hath a thing which thou has fashioned lifted up its head against thee? Verily it shall be overthrown by beneficent words of power, and I will make it to retreat in the sight of thy rays." The holy god opened his mouth and said, "I was walking along the road and passing through the two lands which I myself had created, the two lands of my country when I was bitten by a serpent which I did not see. I am colder than water, I am hotter than fire, all my members sweat, I myself quake, mine eye is unsteady. I cannot look at the heavens and water forces itself on my face as in the time of the inundation."

Figure 12: Images of Aset and Ra from historical Ancient Egyptian Iconography

And Aset said to Ra, "Oh my Divine Father, tell me thy name, for whoever is able to pronounce his name liveth." Ra replied, "I am the maker of the heavens and the earth, I have knitted together the mountains, and I have created everything which exists upon them. I am the maker of the waters (Primeval Ocean), and I have made Meht-ur to come into being; I have made the Bull of his Mother, and I have made the joys of love (love-making) to exist. I am the maker of heaven, and I have made to be hidden the two gods of the horizon, and I have placed the souls

Mysteries of Isis and Ra

of the gods and goddesses within them. I am the being who opens his eyes and the light comes forth; I am the being who shuts his eyes and there is darkness. I am the being who gives the command, and the waters of Hapi (the Nile) burst forth. I am the being whose name the gods and goddesses know not. I am the maker of the hours and the creator of the days. I am the opener (i.e., inaugurator) of the festivals and the maker of the floods of water. I am the creator of the fire of life whereby the works of the houses are caused to come into being. I am Kheper (Khepera) in the morning, Ra at the time of culmination (i.e., noon), and Temu in the evening."

Even though Ra said these great and wonderful things the poison was not driven from its course, and the great God felt no improvement in his condition. Then Aset said to Ra,

"Among the things which you have said to me thy name has not been mentioned. Oh declare it unto me and the poison shall come forth for the person who hath declared his name shall live." Then Ra said, "I will allow myself to be searched through by Aset, and my name shall come forth from my body and go into hers." Then the divine one hid himself from the gods and goddesses, and the throne in the Boat of Millions of Years was empty. And it came to pass that when it was the time for the heart to come forth [from the god], she said unto her son Heru: "The great God is bound by an oath to give his two eyes." Thus, the great god yielded up his name, and Aset, the Great Lady of enchantments, said, "Flow on, poison, and come forth from Ra; let the Eye of Horus come forth from the god and illumine all things outside of his mouth. I have worked, and I make the poison to fall on the ground, for the venom has been mastered. Verily the name hath been taken away from the great god. Let Ra live, and let the poison die, and if the poison lives then Ra shall die. And similarly, a certain man, the son of a certain man, shall live and the poison shall die." These were the words which spoke Aset, the Great Lady, the mistress of the gods, and she had knowledge of Ra in his own name. The above words shall be said over an image of Temu, Heru-Hekennuu, Aset or Heru.

Figure 13: Images of Statues of Aset and Ra

Mysteries of Isis and Ra

Verse 1.

1.1. *Medtu-dj in* Ast   ay   un   m   sa - k
1.2. Words spoken by Aset coming   being in form protection -thine
1.3. These words are spoken by Goddess Isis: "I come to you in a role as your protector

Verse 2.

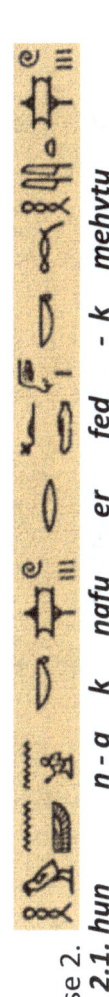

2.1. hun   n - a   k   nafu   er   fed   - k   mehytu
2.2. rejuvenation blow of I thee liberating air for cleansing nose yours, fullness
2.3. I blow, from me to you, the liberating and rejuvenating air from the north, with fullness of consciousness, which cleanses your nose,

Verse 3.

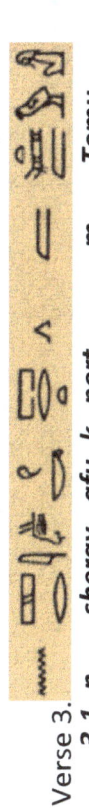

3.1. n   sheray- afu -k pert   m   Temu
3.2. the nostrils [for] body part yours comes in form of Temu
3.3. to the nostrils for your body. This air comes in the form of the god Temu, who is in the north, which is the spirit essence of Ra, the source and sustenance of all life and the successful completion of the spiritual journey.

Mysteries of Isis and Ra

Verse 4.

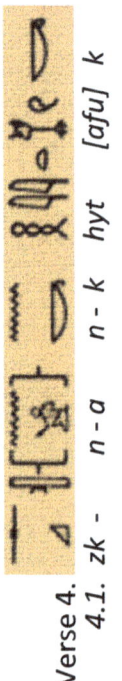

4.1. zk -   n - a   n - k   hyt   [afu] k

4.2. Gathered   to/by me to/for - thee throat body part thine

4.3. I have collected the pieces of your throat for you so you can breathe and live. I pieced your throat back together and cleared obstructions to the air from Temu that conveys the vital life force. So now you have the capacity to experience unobstructed vitality; now you do not have internal obstructions to existing as a conscious living being.

Verse 5.

5.1. erdy   n - a   un   n - k   to thee   m   Neter

5.2. given   from I   being   to thee   in the form of   Divine

5.3. I have given to you the capacity to exist in the form of a God and

Verse 6.

6.1. cheftiu   k   cher   khert   teby   k

6.2. enemies   thine   presence   fall   under   sandals   thine

6.3. in your presence, I present to you your enemies which have fallen under your feet. So now you do not have external obstructions to existing in your divine form.

Verse 7.

7.1. *z - maa   kheru   k   m   nut   usertu   ma   neteru*

7.2. *causes true of speech thine   in   heaven   powers/dominion   behold   gods and goddesses*

7.3. By doing these things, I, the goddess of intuitional wisdom, the embodiment of wisdom, have caused for you to have a divine state in heaven, over which you have power and dominion and all the gods and goddesses behold you!"

SCRIPTURE OF THE MYTH OF ASET AND RA

The Legend of Ra and Aset is contained in the Corpus of Turin Papyri

Section of the Corpus of Turin Papyri

Legend of Ra and Aset found in section -Papyrus de Turin, pll. 31, 77, 131-138.

---

[11] – Translation by Muata Ashby ©2015-2016

SECTION: 1- [Verse 1] SHEDY OF WISDOM AND ASET MEDITATION-LISTENING TO THE TEAACHING PART 1- CREATION AND THE CREATOR

Verse 1.

	Ra	n	Neter	Neterty[12]	kheperu	djesf	ari
1.1.	Ra						
1.2.	Words[13]	of	Divinity	dual divinity	Creator	self	doer/maker

1.3. This scripture is about a Divinity who possesses dual consciousness, who is Creator of itself & creator

Verse 2.

	pet	ta	mau[14]	n	ankh[15]	chet[16]
2.1.	pet	ta	mau	n	ankh	chet
2.2.	heaven	earth	wind/air	of	life	fire

2.3. of heaven and earth and the life force that enlivens Creation, the life giving properties in air that allows the breath of life to sustain life, the fire that enlivens everything,

---

[12] Neterty – divinity possessing dual consciousness, possessing two eyes-of Heru and Ra [moon and sun] i.e. time and space/transcendental insight, relative/absolute, physical, non-physical
[13] Chapter, writings, document.

[14] The term mau also relates to a pun on the letters m-a-u which in a different context relate to cats and lions and that relates us to the feline, leonine energies represented by the goddesses Sekhemit and Bastet, known as sekhem life force. Therefore, mau is "extendedly" defined as the life force in air that when breathed acts as a fire that sustains life.

[15] Also-seruy –breath of life two nostrils and symbol of fire / Nafu n ankh "air/wind of life" as in the air that Aset blew on the body of Asar to revive him.

[16] Akhut –spirit fire

Mysteries of Isis and Ra

Verse 3.

Neteru   remteju   autu[17]   menmenu   djedftu
Gods and goddesses, men and women, animals,   cattle   reptiles

3.1.
3.2. gods and goddesses, of men and women and all four legged creatures, cattle and animals of the farm and all forms of
3.3. reptiles that crawl the earth,

Verse 4.

apedu   remu   suten   remteju   neteru   m
birds   fish.   Royal Lord (of) people (&) gods and goddesses in

4.1.
4.2.
4.3. flying creatures and creatures of the sea as well. This God is king over people and also of gods and goddesses in

Verse 5.

ua[18]   hentyu   er   renpetu   asha   renu
condition/existing oneness   periods 120 years   (are) as to(like) years   many   names

5.1.
5.2.
5.3. a form of oneness whereby it experiences periods of 120 years as though they are one year, who has many names
which are

---

[17] Autu- Four legged animals - ![glyph] , aut -person who is beatlike

[18] ![glyph] secher –condition, state, plan of being or design of existence.

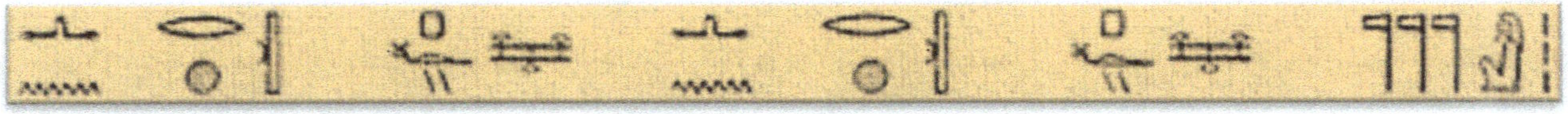

Mysteries of Isis and Ra

Verse 6.

6.1.	*an*	*rech*	*pefy*	*an*	*rech*	*pefy*	*neteru*
6.2.	not	known	this (being).	Not	known	this (being) (to)	gods and goddesses

6.3. not known. The names are not known even to the gods and goddesses!

SECTION: 2- [Verse 7] LISTENING TO THE TEACHING PART 2-UNDERSTANDING THE TROUBLE OF LIFE, DISPASSION, DETACHMENT & CHOICE OF LIFE PATH

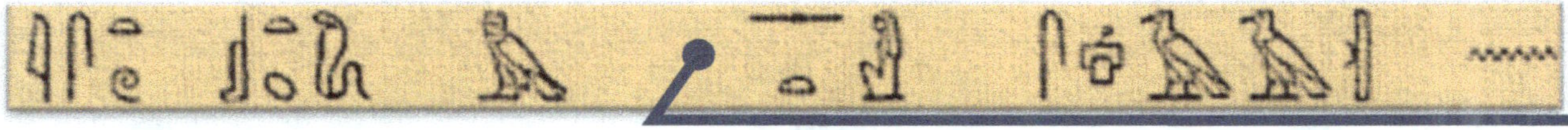

Verse 7.

7.1.	*Astu*	*Aset*	*m*	*zet*	*saa*	*n*
7.2.	Consider	Isis	form	woman	wise	about

7.3. Look, here comes Isis in the form of a physical woman who is also expert on the subject of

Note 1
Aset Listened

Figure 14: Review-Listening Reflection and Meditation from 2007 Neterian Conference

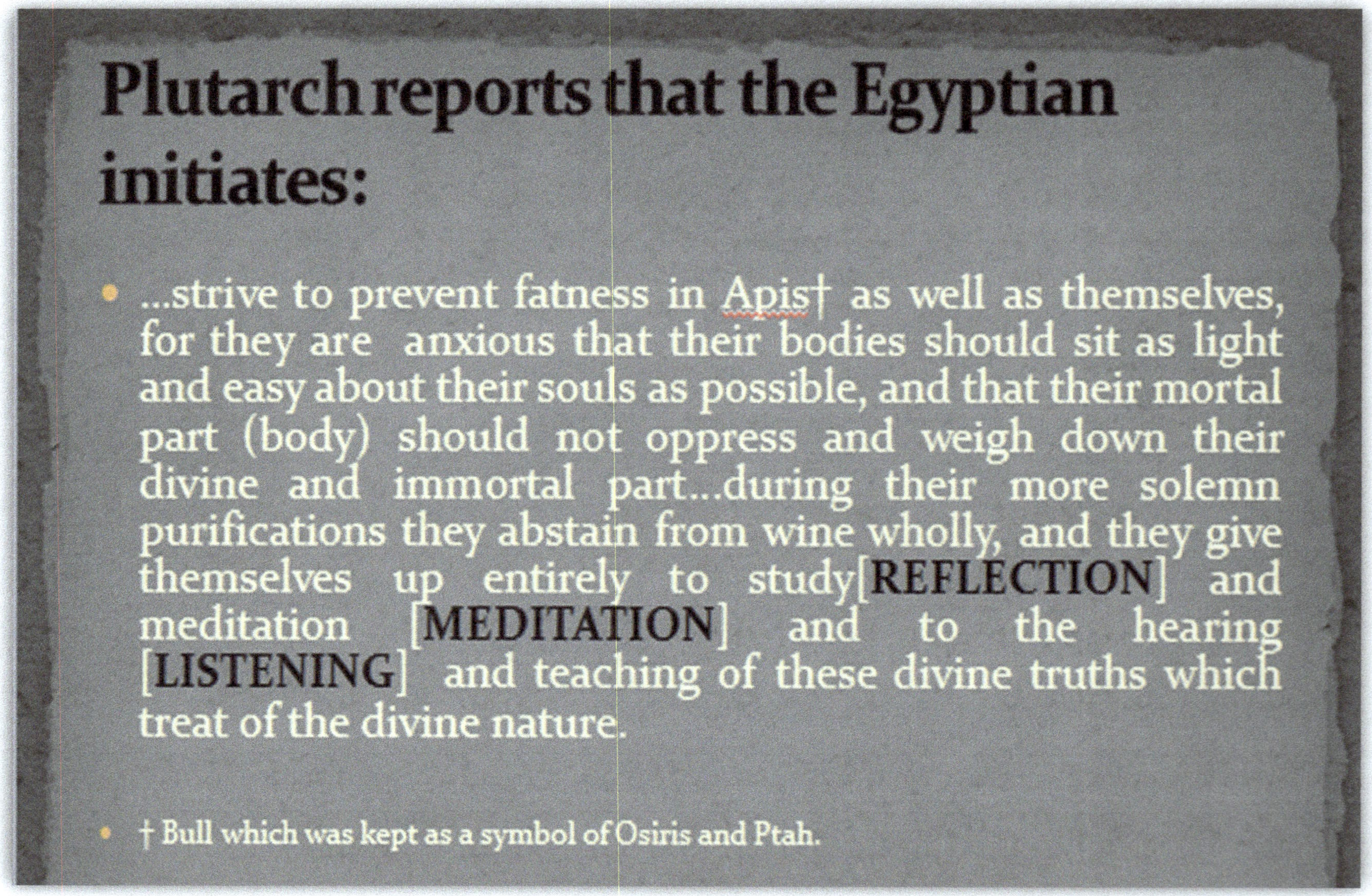
Plutarch reports that the Egyptian initiates:
...strive to prevent fatness in Apis† as well as themselves, for they are anxious that their bodies should sit as light and easy about their souls as possible, and that their mortal part (body) should not oppress and weigh down their divine and immortal part...during their more solemn purifications they abstain from wine wholly, and they give themselves up entirely to study[REFLECTION] and meditation [MEDITATION] and to the hearing [LISTENING] and teaching of these divine truths which treat of the divine nature.
† Bull which was kept as a symbol of Osiris and Ptah.

Mysteries of Isis and Ra

Verse 8.

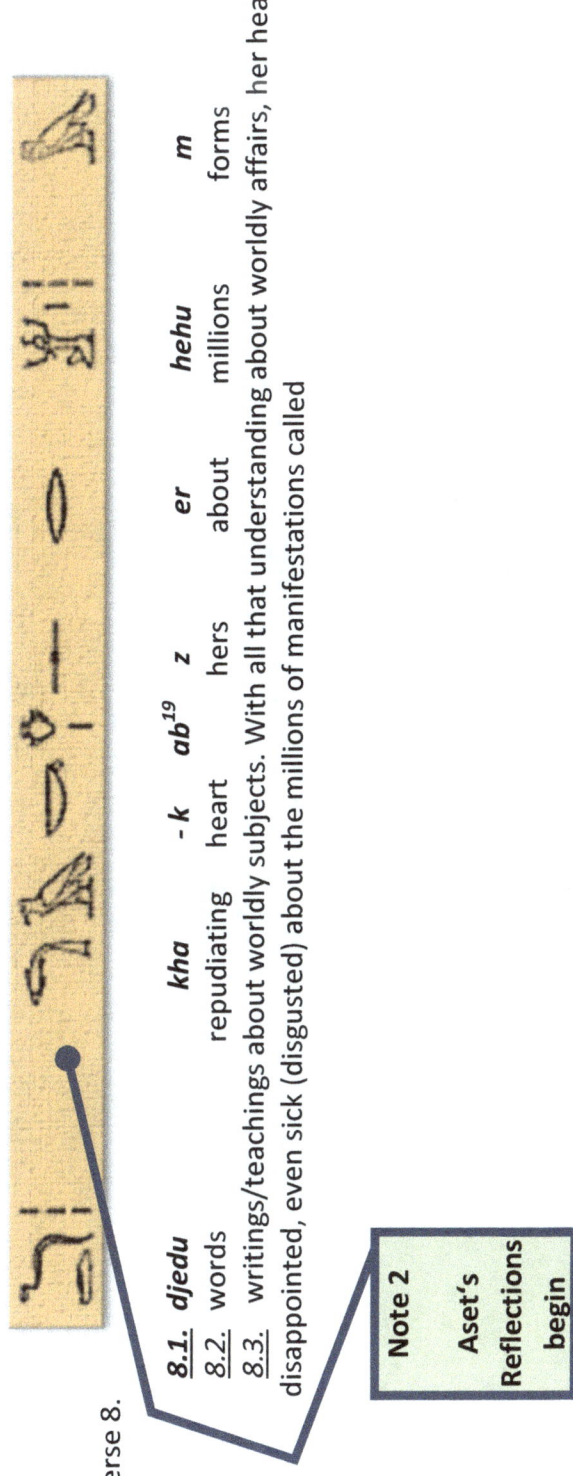

8.1. *djedu*   *kha*   *-k*   *ab*[19]   *z*   *er*   *hehu*   *m*
8.2.   words   repudiating   heart   hers   about   millions   forms
8.3.   writings/teachings about worldly subjects. With all that understanding about worldly affairs, her heart was disappointed, even sick (disgusted) about the millions of manifestations called

Note 2
Aset's Reflections begin

Verse 9.

9.1. *remteju*   *setep res*   *hehu*   *m*   *neteru*   *apt – set*
9.2.   people   choosing instead   millions   forms   gods and goddesses   assessing she
9.3.   of human beings, their activities and futile pursuits. After evaluating the prospect of living life as an ordinary human being she became dispassionate and disillusioned about that; She considered the options of millions of gods and goddesses as better. After she made an assessment of that option

---

[19] Other usages: despicable, accursed, foe, enemy, - form of Apep

Mysteries of Isis and Ra

Verse 10.

10.1. hehu — m — akhu — shepsu — an — khemn — set — m — pet
millions — form — spiritualized venerable/holy ones, not ignorant — she — in — heavenly realm

10.2. she then reconsidered, what about the millions of enlightened sages and saints, what if instead of being an ordinary

10.3. mortal woman she were instead to be like them, not being spiritually ignorant in the heavenly plane

Verse 11.

11.1. ta — mi — Ra — ari — gert — ta
earth plane, — like — Ra — Doing — appropriation — earth

11.2. or ignorant while on earth. In effect be like Ra? That is, to become divine as he, a divinity as he by appropriating for

11.3. myself the divine knowledge as he has? And then she thought: "while on earth, even while alive I could be a

Mysteries of Isis and Ra

SECTION 3: [VERSE 12] ASET'S EARLY REFLECTIONS, MEDITATIONS AND CONCLUSIONS

Verse 12.

> **Note 3**
>
> Here begin Aset's Meditations

Netert	**ka**[20]	**set**	**m**	**ab**[21] **– set**	**er**	**cher/rech**[22]
Goddess?	Reflecting	she	in	heart- hers	as to	wisdom

12.1. Netert — Goddess?
12.2. ka — Reflecting
12.3. Aset thought deeply about the issue (concentration), then more deeply, now going into the depths of her own heart (meditation) and concluded it should be possible to accomplish this lofty goal by becoming wise as to the

Verse 13.

Ren	**Neter**	**shepsy**
Name	Divine	saintly / sanctified / virtuous?

13.1. Ren — Name
13.2. Neter — Divine
13.3. Divine name of Ra, the exalted name, the saintly, virtuous spiritual name of Ra?

---

[20] ka – conscious mind and desires
Kaiu – thoughts
Ka ab –deep thought in the heart,
kaat ab – meditation, mind and feelings in the heart

[21] ab {mind-repository of unconscious impressions=aryu} ariu- {actions, deeds, unconscious mental impressions that impel the desires of the mind}
[22] Scribal error for cher (before or in front of) for rech knowledge

SECTION: 3-STUDY ON THE NATURE OF RA (CREATION)

Verse 14.

14.1. *Astu   aq   n   Ra   ra - neb   m   hat   qetu*

14.2. Observe coming in   is   Ra   day – every   as   head sailors divine

14.3. Consider now Ra comes on the scene, sailing in his boat (sundisk) along with his nine gods and goddesses, who are sailors in his boat, as he does every day coursing through the sky.

Figure 15: Artist rendition of Image of the boat of Ra from contemporary papyrus[23]

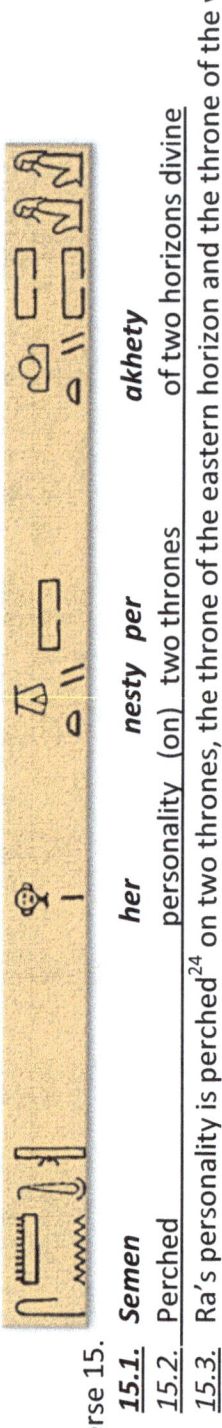

Verse 15.

15.1. *Semen   her   nesty   per   akhety*

15.2. Perched   personality (on) two thrones   of two horizons divine

15.3. Ra's personality is perched[24] on two thrones, the throne of the eastern horizon and the throne of the western horizon; so at this stage he is known as *Ra-Herakhty*, Ra of the two Horizons.

---

[23] From right to left: Ra Hrakhty, Heru, Tem, Shu, Tefnut, Geb, Nut, Asar, Aset, Suten-Neb-Tawi, the Royal Personality (manifestation of Heru on earth.
[24] any temporary resting place for a person or thing

Mysteries of Isis and Ra

Verse 16.

16.1.   **Aaut**   **netery**   **nenu**   **n–f**   **ra**   **f**
       Old age   the divinity dual   drooling/dribbling   is - he   mouth   his

16.2.

16.3. The Divine one, of the two horizons, had become old and had to leave his perches and head for the western horizon of heaven. As he moved along, shuffling with his walking stick, he started dribbling from his mouth.

Verse 17.

17.1. satet[25]   **f**   **he**   **nebau**   **tf**   **er**   **Ta**
       fluid pours   (from)   he   emanation dropping   (from) he[26]   as to   earth

17.2.

17.3. Old age has struck Ra who at this stage is now called Ra Tem. He is as if an arrow has pierced his mature midday Ra-Herakhty form. His drooling/dribbling has now turned into fluid pouring out of his body, the emanations of which are dropping on the earth below as he courses through the sky towards the end of the day.

---

[25] satet   —to become weak, trembling /   cow skin pierced by arrow - injury
[26] He the father (of the gods and goddesses)

Mysteries of Isis and Ra

SECTION: 4 - [Verse 18] SHEDY OF ACTION & DEVOTION (EMOTION) TO GOD IN FORM OF RA-TEM; A RITUAL OBSERVANCE IN LATE AFTERNOON, DEVOTIONAL REMEMBRANCE & MEDITATION, VIEWING RA AND COLLECTING RA'S LIFE FORCE EMANATIONS TO BUILD CONCENTRATION ON RA & SPIRITUAL STRENGTH FOR ONE-POINTEDNESS OF MIND ON THE FORMS, MOVMENTS AND ACTIONS OF RA

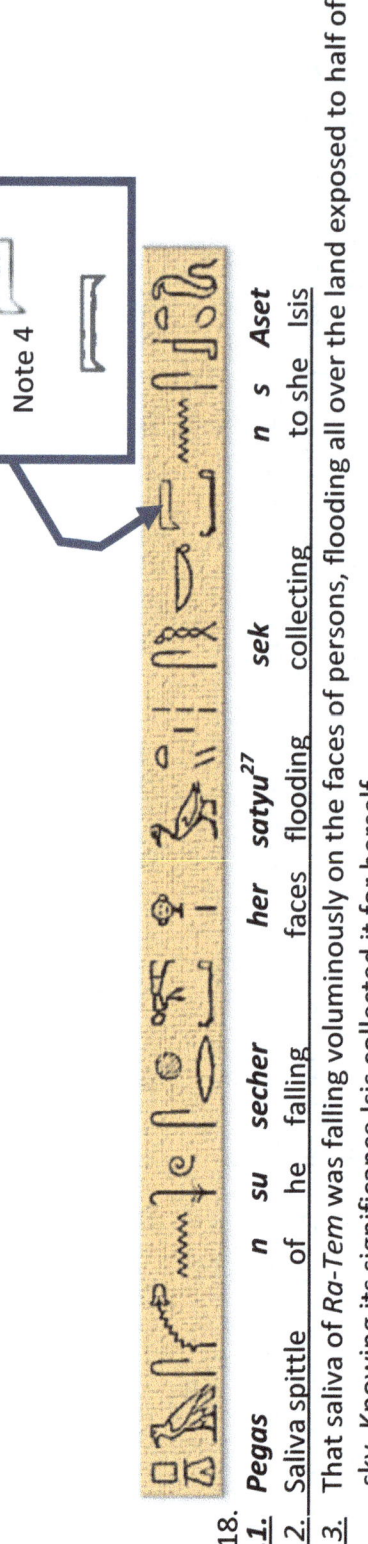

Verse 18.

18.1. *Pegas   n   su   secher   her   satyu*[27]   *sek   n   s   Aset*
Saliva spittle   of   he   falling   faces   flooding   collecting   to she   Isis

18.2.

18.3. That saliva of *Ra-Tem* was falling voluminously on the faces of persons, flooding all over the land exposed to half of the sky. Knowing its significance Isis collected it for herself,

---

[27] *zatet* ![glyph] pour out water, water something / *zaty* ![glyph] flood, flooding

Mysteries of Isis and Ra

SECTION: 5 – [Verse 19] SHEDY OF ACTION AND RIGHT RITUAL- DISCIPLINE OF WORKING DAY BY DAY – GATHERING SPIRITUAL STRENGTH AND STAMINA =FASHIONING ONESELF INTO THE SACRED SERPENT FOR ONE-POINTED VISION

Verse 19.

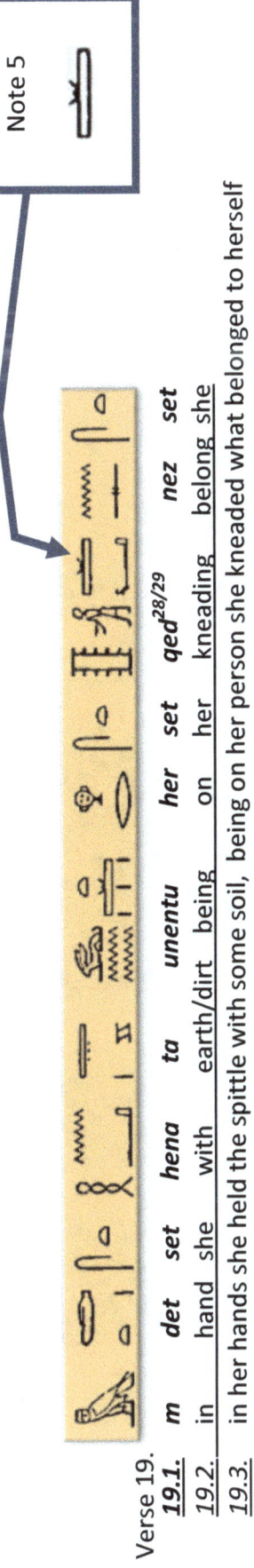

Note 5

19.1. *m   det   set   hena   ta   unentu   her   set   qed*[28/29]   *nez   set*
in   hand   she   with   earth/dirt   being   on   her   kneading   belong   she

19.2.
19.3. in her hands she held the spittle with some soil, being on her person she kneaded what belonged to herself

Verse 20.

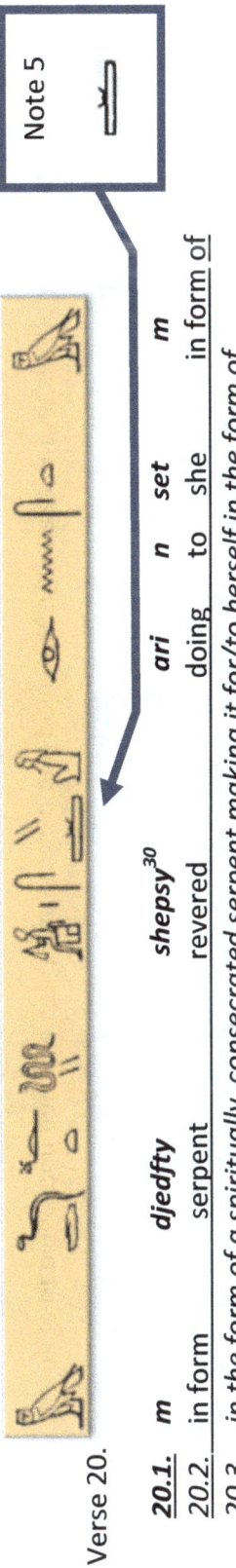

Note 5

20.1.   *m   djedfty*   *shepsy*[30]   *ari   n   set   m*
20.2. in form   serpent   revered   doing   to   she   in form of

20.3. in the form of a spiritually consecrated serpent making it for/to herself in the form of

---

[28] To fashion, construct, build, etc.

[29] rolled scroll tied with string. Significance is profound. Determinative so no phonetic value. Relates to wisdom and what is abstract, conceptual, intangible, ethereal, etc.

[30] ibid

Mysteries of Isis and Ra

Verse 21.

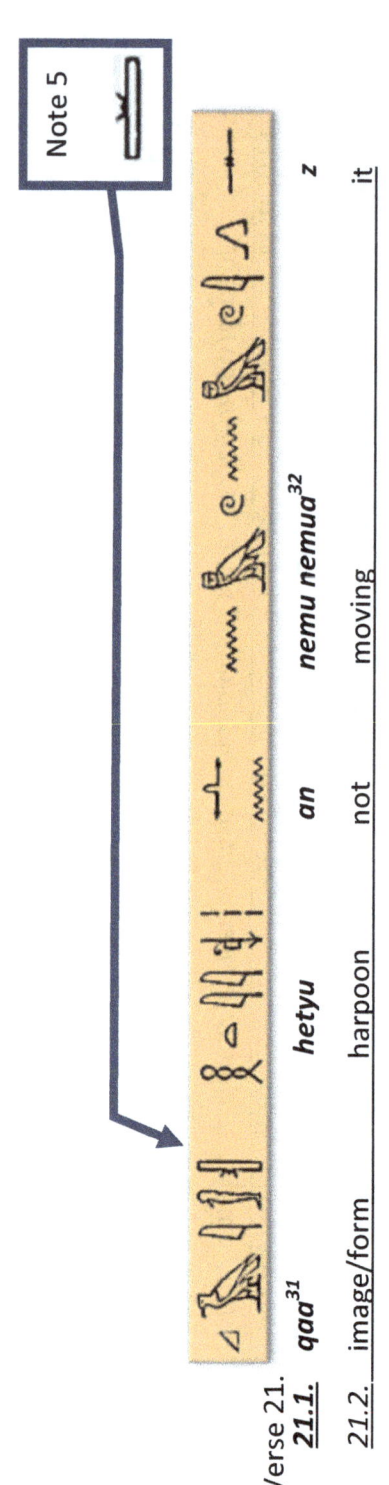

Note 5

21.1.	*qaa*[31]	*hetyu*	*an*	*nemu nemua*[32]	z
21.2.	image/form	harpoon	not	moving	it

21.3.   an image of a harpoon having a shaft that ends in one point but the image of that sacred serpent was not moving yet.

---

[31] ibid

[32] root spelling: 〰🐦〰🐦∧ , nemnem –moving hurriedly. The term nemu is crucial in the teaching of Aset and Ra since at this point the serpent fashioned by Aset is allowed to remain quiet and in this mode its quietness relates to the practice of yogic sleep in which the body becomes paralyzed as during sleep but the meditator remains awake but within the mind; that is, the mind has withdrawn from the externality of the body and into the astral plane of thought where it remains concentrated on one thought or icon (In this case Ra) and instead of expending life force on the external world it retains and builds it in the astral body for the purpose of controling and breaking through the illusoin of Creation. In this case the term relates to movement in serpentine fashion, the way a reptile moves. This implies movements such as wiggling, writhing, twisting, etc.

Mysteries of Isis and Ra

SECTION: 6- [Verse 22] SHEDY OF MEDITATION (CONCENTRATION)-DISCIPLINE OF FOCUS ON RA, THOUGHTS DIRECTED AT THE DIVINE, PATIENCE AND STRIKING AT THE RIGHT TIME

Verse 22.

22.1. **Ankhta**   **er**   **cheft her**   **set**   **chaa**   **set**   **hamu**   **her**

22.2. Alive   as to   before personality   she   went and left   she   lying   upon

22.3. It was alive and in front of her, she then left the area, leaving it lying there on the

Verse 23.

23.1. **wat**   **apep**   **Neter aah**   **her**   **s**

23.2. path   traveled   God Great   heavy/burdened

23.3. path which the Great God in his old age traveled regularly but now feeling heavy, tired and burdened by his old age,

Verse 24.

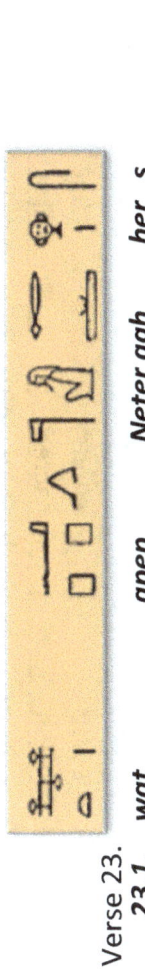

24.1. **er**   **aba**   **ab-f**   **mchet**   **tawy - f**

24.2. as to   desire of heart   his   passing through   two lands his

24.3. but anyway Ra continued on, passing through his two lands as he pleased.

Verse 25.

25.1. **Neter shepsy**   **cha – f**   **er**   **ha**   **neteru**

25.2. Divinity exalted/holy   shining he   as to   behind   gods and goddesses

25.3. This Holy Divinity was still shining even as the gods and goddesses were behind him

Mysteries of Isis and Ra

Verse 26.
26.1. m — aah perty — ankh — udja — senab — mchet – f
in — great double house — life — vitality — health — passing through -he

26.2.

26.3. in the great double house that is the rulership of upper and lower Egypt, with life, vitality and health, be to him, as he continued on moving along.

Verse 27.
27.1. Seft seft - f — mi — Ra neb — unchu — set — m
Stepping — he — like — day every — bite — it/she — in

27.2.

27.3. Striding along as usual, as he did every day along the same path, he was bitten by means of a

Verse 28.
28.1. Djedfty — shepsy — djezef — chet — ankh — perti
Serpent — sacred — himself — fire — life — coming forth

28.2.

28.3. Sacred serpent which bit Ra caused Ra's fire of life to flow out

Verse 29.
29.1. im — f — djezef — der — nez — imy — na — ashu
into — he — himself — overpowered — it (one who) — in — the — cedar

29.2.

29.3. into he himself as he was overpowered by it even as he is now in his domain of cedar.

Mysteries of Isis and Ra

SECTION: 7- [Verse 30] SHEDY OF ASET MEDITATION (WITNESSING & REFLECTING)-DISCIPLINE OF BEHOLDING THE FLUTTER OF CREATION CONFIRMING ITS ILLUSORINESS AS RA & GODS AND GODDESSES FALTER IN MAINTAINING HIS LIFE WHICH SUSTAINS CREATION AFTER BEING BITTEN BY THE SACRED SERPENT

Verse 30.
30.1. *Neter   Neterty   un   -f   Ra   -f   kheru   n*

30.2. Divinity dual divinity   open   he   mouth his speech   by

30.3. This twofold holy being opened his mouth and the speech by

Verse 31.
31.1. *hem - f   ankh udja senab   peh   n-f   er   Pet   Paut*

31.2. majesty he   life, vitality, health arrived to/of he as to heaven   company

31.3. his majesty   life, vitality, health be to him, reached to the heavens.   The company of

Verse 32.
32.1. *neteru   tu – f   her   ma   pu-u   what   thattt   neteru – f*

32.2. gods and goddesses his   persons   gods and goddesses his

32.3. his gods and goddesses   their personalities exclaimed "whats going onnn?" Ra's gods and goddesses

Mysteries of Isis and Ra

Verse 33.
33.1. her   peterau   an   gem   -f
       persons   asking what what?   not   finding   -he
33.2.
33.3. they al asked   what is it? What is it? What's the matter? Ra could not find the

Verse 34.
34.1. medtu   er   ushebt   her –f   arty   sekherui   fy
34.2. words   for   answer   Face his   jaws   his both
34.3. words to describe the problem and his jaws were dropping so he could not speak words to answer their questions

Verse 35.
35.1. her chetchet   atu   -f   neb   astyty   metut
35.2. face rattle   limbs -his   all   trembling   venum/poison
35.3. in his face were chattering and all limbs were trembling because the poison

Mysteries of Isis and Ra

Verse 36.

36.1. *tjetet   n – f   m   aufe   -fy   mi   tjetet   hapi*

36.2. **overwhelming to him in body parts his - bear like overwhelming   God Hapi waters land**

36.3. was overwhelming him, overpowering his entire body just as the Nile River overwhelms the land

 Determinative "construction", "Build wall"   Determinative "water"

Determinative "body of water, lake, sea"   Determinative "piece of land"

Verse 37.

37.1. *m   chet – f   Neter   aah   smenti   n – f   ab – f*

37.2. through vegetation.   The God Great   caused   firmness   to himself   heart his

37.3. and over the vegetation at floodtime. This Great God steeled himself as best he could and calmed his heart from all the stress temporarily

Mysteries of Isis and Ra

Verse 38.

38.1. nas   -f   er   amyu   chet -f   may   tenu   na
called out he   as to   decendants   his   'Come over,   you all   to me

38.2. and he was able to call out to the gods and goddesses that came after him since he brought them into existence, who

38.3. follow and look after him. He said to them: "come over all of you, come to me...

Verse 39.

39.1. khepertu   m   hatu   -a   neteru
creations   in   body   mine   gods and goddesses

39.2.

39.3. all of you, having been created in my body, you gods and goddesses...

Verse 40.

40.1. peru   m   -a   dit   rech   tenu
coming forth   through -me   give knowledge to you all

40.2.

40.3. who come forth from me. I tell you now

Mysteries of Isis and Ra

Verse 41.

<u>41.1.</u> khepera – set   demu   nut   chet   meru

<u>41.2.</u> created - thing   cut   that   thing   painful illness

<u>41.3.</u> some creature cut me or bit me, a thing that bites; it has made me painfully sick

Verse 42.

<u>42.1.</u> rech set   ab – a   an   maa – su   mau - a   an

<u>42.2.</u> know it   heart mine   not   see - it   eyes - mine   not

<u>42.3.</u> Deep down I have no idea whatsoever what it was and neither did my eyes see what it was and it was not

Verse 43.

<u>43.1.</u> ari   z – det – a   an   rech - set   m   ari   n-a   nebt

<u>43.2.</u> made   of - hand - mine   not   know - it   through   done   to me   any

<u>43.3.</u> made by my hand and I don't know by what means or how this was done to me

Mysteries of Isis and Ra

Verse 44.

44.1. an   deptu   ment   mitet – set   an   meru
not   tasted   pain   likeness - it   not   painful illness

44.2. nor have I tasted this kind of pain ever before; this is new to me; I have not expereinced this painful illness or anything like

44.3.

Verse 45.

45.1. er – z   anuk   zer   sa   zer
onto - it   I am   prince/noble   son   prince/noble[33]

45.2. it. How can this be happening to ME!; I am a prince, from noble birth, who is the son of a a noble,

45.3.

Verse 46.

46.1. mu   kheperu   m   Neter.   Anuk   ur
outflow   created   through   Divinity.   I am   great

46.2. an emission created through the Divine Self. I am a great one so this trouble is not supposed to be for me...

46.3.

---

[33] In this context the term "zer" relates to nobility, royalty and specifically to a spiritual royalty. One of the 75 names of Ra is zer aah ⟨glyphs⟩ "Great noble one". The god Asar (Osiris) is similarly referred to. Nevertheless the construction of the sentence means that Ra is not The Ultimate God but a descendant of that Supreme Being.

Mysteries of Isis and Ra

SECTION: 8- [Verse 47] SHEDY OF WISDOM (SEBAIT-PHILOSOPHY)-DISCIPLINE OF UNDERSTANDING THERE IS A SECRET NATURE OF GOD (RA) THAT WAS HITHERTO UNKNOWN AND NEEDS TO BE DISCOVERED IN ORDER TO ATTAIN THE GOAL OF LIFE

Verse 47.

47.1. *sa*   *ur*   *maut*   *n*   *atef*   *ren*

47.2. son/child   great.   Essence   of   father   name

47.3. as I am the son, the offspring of a Great one. The essence of my father is my name.

Verse 48.

48.1. *Anuk*   *ashau*   *renu*   *ashatu*   *kheperu*   *iu*

48.2. I am   many   names   miriad   forms   it is

48.3. I have many names and countless forms that are also my creations; and it is my

Verse 49.

49.1. *khepera - a*   *unu*   *m*   *neter*   *neb*   *nas*   *tu*

49.2. reflections   existing   form   divinity   every.   call out   to

49.3. my reflections I brought into being that manifest in the form of all gods and goddesses. I am declaring this to

Mysteries of Isis and Ra

Verse 50.

50.1. **Temu** **Heru** **Hekenu** *iu* *djed* *atef* *– a*

50.2. Temu Heru Hekenu it is said father -mine

50.3. Temu, the ender of things and to Heru Hekenu who is the singer of divine glories;_ it was spoken by my father

Verse 51.

51.1. *mut – a* *ren – a* *amun – set* *m* *khat – a* *er*

51.2. mother -mine name -mine hidden - it in body -mine as to

51.3. and my mother, my name and it was hidden in my constitution, my very being itself and this was done by

Verse 52.

52.1. *mes – a* *n* *mery* *tem* *erdit* *kheperu* *pehty*

52.2. birthing—me of desire not permit create power[34]

52.3. one who gave birth to me and in accord with their desire it should not be permitted that the name should be divulged, lest be created, might be allowed, that someone gain power

---

[34] Power, strength, might, glory, renown, prominence, notoriety, illustriousness

Mysteries of Isis and Ra

 ***tem*** 1-to finish something, complete something, bring or come to an end; 2-complete, all together, entirety, whole; 3-not allow, not permit, not authorize, not sanction, not approve-i.e. not allow to be completed the acquisition of ultimate dominion over Ra.

Verse 53.

53.1. hekau   – a   n   hekay   er   – a

53.2. words of power - mine   of   words of power commander over – me

53.3. of my secret words that control all Creation and become a personality who can use those words effectively and thereby also be able to use them even over me too.

Mysteries of Isis and Ra

SECTION: 9-SUMMARY 54-61: Ra explains his illness and calls for the Gods and Goddesses who are skillful in healing words of power to come to him from all over Creation.

Verse 54.

54.1. **peru**   **k**   **er**   **ha**   **er**   **maa**   **ari**   **n - a**

54.2. coming   about   location-behind   about   see   made   of -me

54.3. I was cooming forth to see about what was made for me and I meant to stay hidden, out of view, and look at things in Creation in a stealthy manner, without calling attention to myself.

Verse 55.

55.1. **setut**   **m**   **tawy**   **qemamu**   **n - a**

55.2. walking about   in   two lands   created   of/by - me

55.3. I was just trying to take a simple, inconspicuous stroll through the world I created.

Verse 56.

56.1. **m**   **djedm**   **cher - a**   **an**   **rech - a**   **su**

56.2. in   puncture   condition - I   not   know - I   it

56.3. In this way I was stuck or bitten and I was bewildered; I did not have a clue as to what it was.

Mysteries of Isis and Ra

Verse 57.
57.1. an chet   as pu   an   mu   as pu   ab – a   chery
       Not fire   look this   Not   water look this   heart mine having

57.2. Take notice, this feeling is not like fire, not like water. My heart is having

57.3.

Verse 58.
58.1. chetu   hatu - a   astytyu   atu - a   chery
       burning   limbs - mine   shaking   limbs - mine   having

58.2. burning sensations and also in my limbs; and my limbs are shaking uncontrollably as if they contain

58.3.

Verse 59.
59.1. mesu   hesyu
       children   vibrating

59.2. Spawns of those who tremble in fear due to a cold wind blowing through them.

59.3.

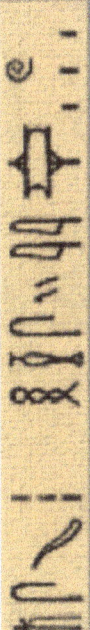

hesy-singing   nafu-wind   = right pitch voice to shatter creation

Mysteries of Isis and Ra

Verse 59.A

59.1. *amma   antu   n - a*
59.2. Give   bring   to/of - me
59.3. May be granted this command, that they be brought to me

Verse 60.

60.1. *mesu   neteru   akhuyu   medtu   rechy*
60.2. children   gods and goddesses   beneficent/vitalizing   words/speech   knowledgeable
60.3. my children, the gods and goddesses who have knowledge of beneficial and healing words of power

Verse 61.

61.1. *er senu   saard   senu   pen senu   her*
61.2. mouths theirs   well-intended   they   arrive they   head heavenly
61.3. in their mouths. May they be well intentioned divinities with good will towards me and may they arrive to their commander, their lord in heaven.

Mysteries of Isis and Ra

SECTION: 10- [Verse 62] SHEDY OF WISDOM-UNDERSTANDING RA AND THE COSMIC FORCES ARE POWERLESS BEFORE THE MIGHT OF A SERIOUS, DISPASSIONATE, RELENTLESS & REGULAR -NOT INTERMITTENT SPIRITUAL ASPIRANT

Verse 62.

62.1. iu   er–f   mesu   neter   neb   im   khery

walking in   about he   children   god   all   in   servant

62.2.

62.3. Coming to see about Ra, his children, all the gods and goddesses, his servants arrived.

Verse 63.

63.1. akebu   n-f   iu   n   Aset   khery   khut   - set

crying   for – him   walking in   is   Isis   servant   power   - she

63.2.

63.3. They were crying at the sight of Ra. Then arrived Isis, also his servant, who was not crying but instead she was provisioned with power

Verse 64.

64.1. aset   ra   set   m   nafu   n   ankh   tjez   - set

abode   mouth she   in   breath   of   life   creative words   - hers

64.2.

64.3. residing in her mouth, in the form of breath of life, her invocatory creative words of power.

Mysteries of Isis and Ra

Verse 65.

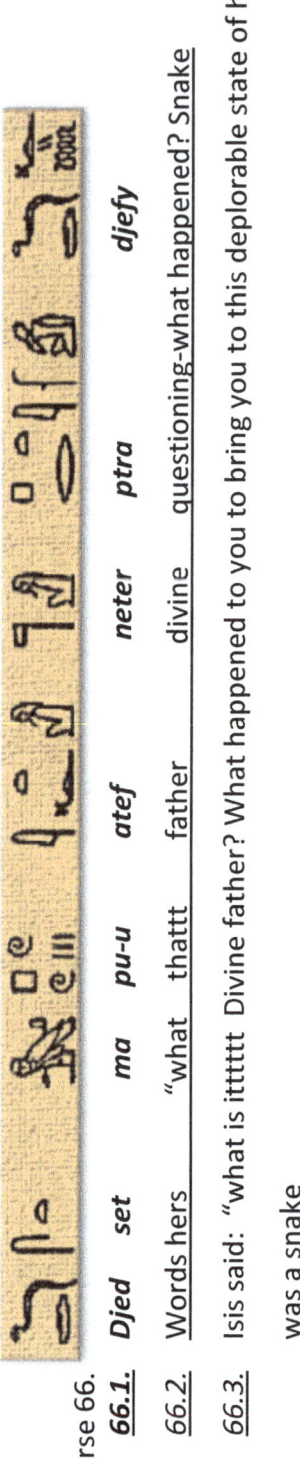

65.1.   *her der mentu medtu - set s–ankh gau hetyu*

65.2.   person overwhelmed unstable words – hers cause –life mucus throats

65.3.   For a person who may be overwhelmed by instability, her words cause life to be restored and dispelling the mucus clogging the throat that is choking and preventing proper breathing as well as the ignorance obstructing the enlightened consciousness.

Verse 66.

66.1.   *Djed set ma pu-u atef neter ptra djefy*

66.2.   Words hers "what thattt father divine questioning-what happened? Snake

66.3.   Isis said: "what is itttttt Divine father? What happened to you to bring you to this deplorable state of health? I think it was a snake

Verse 67.

67.1.   *den menu pa im k ua mes k fa*

67.2.   bit illness present_in thee, one creature thine rose up

67.3.   that bit you and caused this illness to happen in you. It was done by one of your creatures, a creature of your own creation that reared up

Mysteries of Isis and Ra

Verse 68.

68.1.   *dep f*   *er – k*   *ka*   *scher*   *set*   *m*

      head his   against -thee   certainly   fall   it   through

68.3. its head in defiance of you. No matter, its attack will stop by means of

Verse 69.

69.1.   *hekayu*   *menchu*   *di - a*   *chetchet*   *-a*   *-f*   *-he*   *er*

      words of power   corrective   give - I   march away – I   -he   as to

69.3. corrective and restorative, curative words of power. I will provide them and the illness, he shall march away like a

defeated army so that

Verse 70.

70.1.   *maa*   *saty*   *k*   *Neter*   *djeser*   *wepu*   *n-f*   *ra*   *f*

      sight   rays   thine Divinity   exhalted   opened   to-he   mouth   his

70.3. it will be gone from the sight of your rays.   This sublime Divinity opened his mouth:

SECTION: 11-SUMMARY 71-78: SHEDY OF ACTION AND WISDOM (ANTET BEGAG) NOT BEING DECIEVED BY RA AND HIS ILLUSORY CREATION

Verse 71.

71.1. Anuk   pu shemy   her   wat   sutut   m

71.2. I was   this walking along   upon   path   traveling   in

71.3. All I was doing was walking along; that's it, I wasn't looking for trouble or causing any harm, just trekking on the path I usually travel on through

Verse 72.

72.1. tawy   zemtet -a   aba   n   ab a   er   maa

72.2. two lands   country -I   desire   of   heart mine   about   see

72.3. the lands of upper and lower Egypt, my own country. My heart desired to go about on the path so I could see

Verse 73.

73.1. qemamu   n – a   chunn   n -a   m   djed-fy

73.2. created   for –me   bite   to – me   through   serpent

73.3. the things I had created of myself. Then I was bitten by means of a serpent.

Mysteries of Isis and Ra

Verse 74.

74.1. *an maa set   an chet as pu   an mu as pu*
not see it   not fire like this   not water look this

74.2. I did not see it. Take notice, it doesn't feel like fire or like water, neither hot nor cold; nor one way or the other, but

74.3. something in between, something beyond that duality.

Verse 75.

75.1. *qebeb   kua   er   mu   shemem   kua   er*
cold   I am   compared   water   hot   I am   compared

75.2.

75.3. I am colder than the temperature of water and hotter than the temperature of

Verse 76.

76.1. *chet   hatu   a   neb   er   khery   fetetu   tua*
fire   limbs   mine   all   about   possessing   sweat   me

76.2.

76.3. fire and my limbs are all dripping with sweat coming out from me and they are

Mysteries of Isis and Ra

Verse 77.

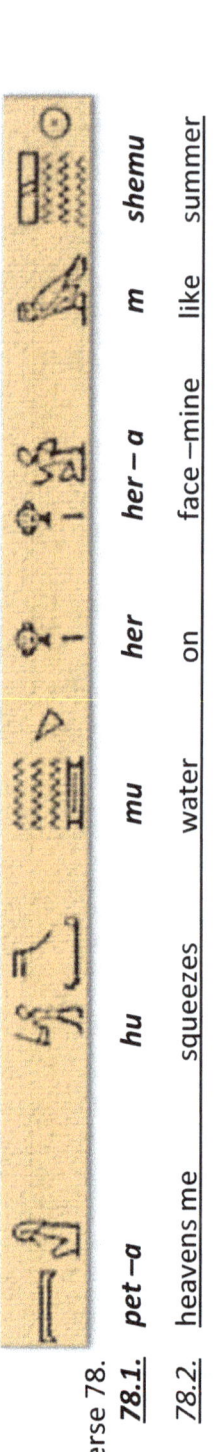

77.1. *astyty aritet an smenti an gemhu - a*

77.2. trembling eyes not steady not perceiving - I

77.3. trembling. My eyes are unsteady and I cannot see my surroundings clearly; I am dizzy and I cannot perceive

Verse 78.

78.1. *pet – a hu mu her her – a m shemu*

78.2. heavens me squeezes water on face –mine like summer

78.3. the heavenly region of my own creation. It feels as if water is being squeezed onto my face just as happens in the heat of the summer time.

Mysteries of Isis and Ra

SECTION: 12- [Verse 79] SHEDY OF ACTION AND WISDOM AND MEDITATION (LASER FOCUS ON GOAL OF LIFE) ASET UNDETERRED, ASKS RA FOR HIS NAME – WITH SPECIAL WORDS OF POWER-AS A CONDITION OF PROVIDING THE CURE

Verse 79.

79.1. *Djed in Aset*   *Aa!*   *Djed n-a ren –a k*
79.2. Words by Isis   to Ra   hey!   Tell to me name (divine) yours
79.3. These words were spoken by Isis. "Tell me your name

Verse 80.

80.1. *Atef Neter Neter ankh*   *z-a*   *demu tu her*
80.2. Father divine divine life   to -one   affirms the personality's
80.3. Divine Father, the divine name. There is life to one who affirms their personality's

Verse 81.

81.1. *ren –f anuk*   *ari*   *pet ta*
81.2. name his I am   maker/creator   heaven earth
81.3. name." (Reply by Ra:) "I am the Creator of the heavenly realm and the earthly realm

Mysteries of Isis and Ra

Verse 82.

| 82.1. | *tjezu* | *duu* | *qemamu* | *un-en* | *tenu* | *her* | *f* |
| 82.2. | knitter | mountains | Creating | existence of things | on | he |

82.3. interweaver/constructor/knotter of the mountains and all physical creation. One, who puts together, interconnects and creates things and brings them into existence on himself.

Mysteries of Isis and Ra

SECTION: 13-Summary V83-93: SHEDY OF ACTION, MEDITATION, WISDOM-RELENTLESS INSISTANCE, (ANTET BEGAG) AND NOT BEING DISUADED -AFTER BEING ASKED ABOUT HIS NAME RA TRIES TO, IN A FUTILE EFFORT, TO DISUADE ASET BY OFFERING MORE MISINFORMATION ABOUT HIS NATURE AND NAME- CULMINATING IN THE PROCLAMATION OF HIS THREE MAIN FORMS

Verse 83.

83.1. *Nuk*   *ari*   *mu*   *khepertu*

83.2. I am   maker   waters   bringer eistence

83.3. I am the maker of the waters of Creation and the one who brought into existence

Verse 84.

84.1. *Mehyt*   *-ur*   *ari*   *ka*   *-n*   *-mut*   *f*   *kheperu*

84.2. flood   great   doer   Bull   of   mother   His   Creator

84.3. the Great Flood, that mighty fullness that fills Creation itself. I am the one who acts as the one who engenders Creation

by impregnating his own body, just as a bull impregnates many cows; also I am creator of

Mysteries of Isis and Ra

Verse 85.

85.1. nedjemnedjemyu nuk ari pet zshetatu

all pleasures. I am maker heavens cause mysteries

85.3. of the pleasures of life, the feelings of joy, happiness and sexual delights. I am the fabricator of the heavens and the one who is the source of the mysteries of the

Verse 86.

86.1. akhety dit -a ba nu neteru m khenu set

two horizon divinity. Give - I soul of gods and goddesses through inside it

86.3. divinity of the two horizons, Heru m akhet (Heru of the two horizons), that Ra Herakhty, (Ra of the two Horizons), the being who is of two worlds and dual existence. I am the one who gives souls to all the gods and goddesses and places it within each of their bodies.

Verse 87.

87.1. Nuk un arty – f kheperu hedjdjutu

87.2. I am open eyes – his Bringer into existence shining light

87.3. I am the one that when he opens his eyes there is the shining of light that comes into existence, the light that shines all over the earth.

Mysteries of Isis and Ra

Verse 88.

88.1. Achnnu   arty -f   kheperu   kekuy   hu

88.2. Closing   eyes   Bringer into existence   darkness   squeeze

88.3. There comes about darkness upon closing my eyes. I am the one responsible for squeezing, pushing along,

Verse 89.

89.1. Hapi   cheft   udu   n -f

89.2. the Nile river   according to when   commanded by he.

89.3. the Nile river in accord with the commands of its commander.

Verse 90.

90.1. An   rech   n   neteru   ren   f   Nuk   ari   unu

90.2. Not known   by   gods and goddesses   name   Divine   his   I am   maker   hours

90.3. The gods and goddesses do not know my real name. I am the maker of time itself.

Verse 91.

91.1. Kheperu   heru   Nuk   wepu   hebu   renpt

91.2. Bringer into existence   days.   I am   opener   festivals   year

91.3. I am also the one who brings days into existence. I am as well the opener of festivals and annual rituals.

Mysteries of Isis and Ra

Verse 92.
92.1. | Qemamu | atru | Nuk | ari |
| Creator | water ways. | I am | maker |

92.2.

92.3. I am the Creator of rivers, lakes, the flooding of the Nile basin, seas and oceans; I am behind all those things. I am the maker of

Verse 93.
93.1. | chet | ankht | er | s-kheperu | katu | n | amtu |
| fire | life | as to | causing coming into existence | labors | of | buildings. |

93.2.

93.3. the fire of life, the life force, the energy which is used in causing the coming into being of works that go on in warehouses, homes, offices and all buildings.

Verse 94.
94.1. | Nuk | Khepra | m | dauu | Ra | m | ahau - f |
| I am | Khepera | in | morning, | Ra | in | noon he, |

94.2.

94.3. I am Khepera the creator in the morning and I am Ra the sustainer at noon,

Mysteries of Isis and Ra

Verse 95.
- **95.1.** *Temu* *imy* *masheru* *an* *khesef*
- **95.2.** *Temu* *in* *evening* *not* *forced*
- **95.3.** and Temu the completer, in the evening. After all the things he said there was no effect

Verse 96.
- **96.1.** *metut* *m* *shemi* *set* *an* *nedjem* *neter* *aah*
- **96.2.** *poison* *as* *travel* *it* *not* *comforted* *god* *great*
- **96.3.** on the poison that was killing Ra and it did not go marching away out of his body like a defeated army. So Ra, the great god, was not relieved of his pain at all.

SECTION: 14 - [Verse 97] SHEDY OF ACTION WISDOM FOCUS AND NON-STOP (RELENTLESS) INSISTANCE (AN CHEN) - WITHOUT STOPPING HER EFFORTS

Verse 97.

97.1. Djed in Aset n Ra An ren k ipu

97.2. *Speech by Isis to Ra. Not name thine listed*

97.3. Then Isis said to Ra: "in all those things you told me, the whole catalog of things you itemized, I did not hear your name

Verse 98.

98.1. m na djedu k n-a A djed k thee setu it n-a to me

98.2. *in the words thine to me. Oh tell thee it to me*

98.3. anywhere in those words that you told me. Oh Ra, I ask thee again to tell me your Divine name.

Verse 99.

99.1. Pery ta metut ankh z - a

99.2. *Come forth that poison; life to -one*

99.3. The poison is removed and life is restored to a person when they

Mysteries of Isis and Ra

Verse 100.
100.1. demu   tu   ren   -f   metu   djedmu   set
100.2. declares   it   name   -his   poison   burns   it
100.3. affirm it, when they unequivocally state their name!" The poison, it burns

Verse 101.
101.1. m   djedemu   sekhemu   n-z   er   nebau   n
101.2. through burning   power   of-it   as to   flareup   of
101.3. by means of the burning power of its flames that flareup

Mysteries of Isis and Ra

SECTION: 15- [Verse 102] RA RELENTS AND AGREES TO OPEN HIMSELF UP FOR ASET TO ENTER HIM AND DISCOVER HIS REAL NAME-HERE ENDS THE LOWER MEDITATION PRACTICE AND THE GOAL OF THE SACRED SERPENT HAS BEEN ACHIEVED-DISARMING RA (CREATION) AND ALLOWING ITS ESSENTIAL NATURE TO BE DISCOVERED BY JOINING WITH IT. SO AT THIS POINT THERE ARE NO MORE THOUGHTS< CHANT OR CONCENTRATION OR FOCUS ON THE IMAGES OF RA

Verse 102.

102.1. art   Djed   in   Hem   n   Ra   dit   n - a

102.2. fire/heat   Speech by   majesty   of   Ra: "give of me

102.3. of the destructive heat. His majesty, Ra, said: "Alright, I give up. I freely give myself over

Verse 103.

103.1. hehuty - a   ma   Aset   pert   ren - a   m

103.2. open/inspection - I for   Isis.   Come forth   name -   mine   in

103.3. to be looked through without obstruction. My name shall come forth which is in

Verse 104.

104.1. khat a - er   khat - z   Amun   n   su   netery   m

104.2. body mine - to   body - hers. Hidden   of   he   divine self   in

104.3. my body and it shall pass to the body of Isis, for it cannot be spoken wihth words since there are no words that can describe it or contain it. Having said that, the divine being, Ra became hidden within

Mysteries of Isis and Ra

Figure 16: Tem in his boat and then absent

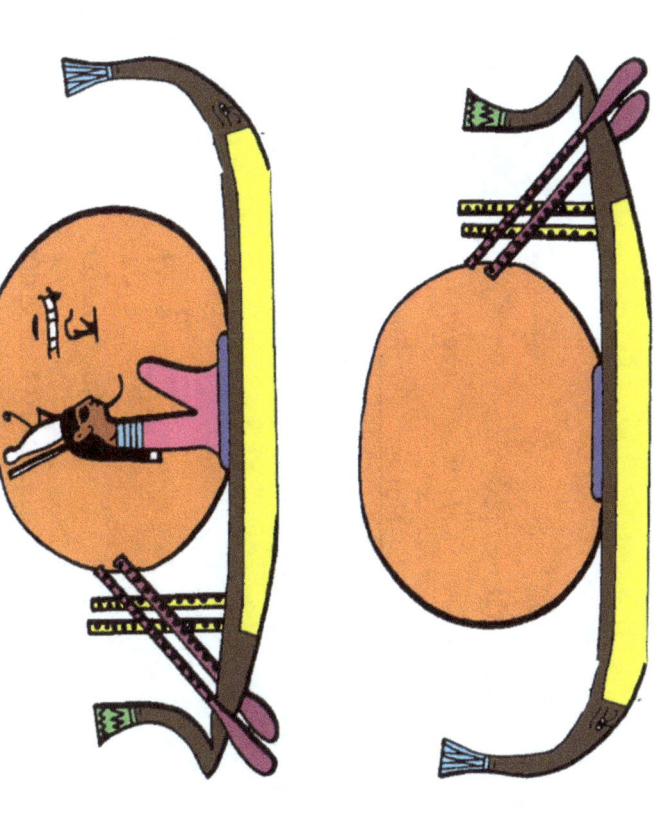

Verse 105.

neteru	usech	aset	m	uia	n	hehu
105.1. gods goddesses;	empty	throne	in	boat	of	millions

105.2. his gods and goddesses. His throne in the boat of millions of years was empty and he was not to be seen. Ra-Tem retreated into the gods and goddesses his Creation. Having succeeded through the last test of will Aset went past the illusory Creations of Ra and now also past his illusory identity as embodied Divine personality, entering a void of undifferentiated consciousness (Anrutef) in which is to be found the source of all Ra's divinity and thus becoming one with the essence of that which is described as the Father/Mother divine, I,e, Neter, the undefined, transcendental divine.

105.3.

Mysteries of Isis and Ra

SECTION: 1- [Verse 106] HAVING ACHIEVED THE GOAL TEMU'S THRONE IS VACANT AND HE IS NO LONGER THE SOLE RULER OF CREATION. ASET MADE A PACT WITH RA TO USE HER INTUITIONAL WISDOM TO PROVIDE THE TEACHING OF ENLIGHTENMENT TO HERU WHEN IT'S TIME TO COME FORTH (ENLIGHTENMENT)

Verse 106.

106.1. *Ar*   *kheperu*   *mi*   *zep*   *pert*   *net*

106.2. As to   creation   like   time   coming forth   of

106.3. As regard to a time that will come in the future, a time that is created like the time of the first creation when there will be coming forth of

Verse 107.

107.1. *ab*   *djed*   *z*   *n*   *sa*   *Heru*   *zenhau*   *net*   *su*

107.2. heart   words   hers   to   son   Horus   binding   of   he

107.3. the heart as is described in the Pert M Heru –the "Book of Coming Forth and becoming Heru" for that time, due to what has been done here now; let there be a compact with him (between Ra and Heru)

Verse 108.

108.1. *m*   *ankh*   *neter*   *erdat*   *neter*   *maa*   *fy*

108.2. in   life oath   divinity   gives   divine   eyes his both

108.3. in a life oath with the divinity, that when the time comes the Divinity (Ra) will give his two eyes.

Mysteries of Isis and Ra

SECTION: 16– Verses 109-114-RA'S NAME OFFICIALLY DISCOVERED-ASET DECLARES SHE WILL CURE RA AND BANISH THE POISON ALLOWING HIS HEALTH AND VISION

Verse 109.

109.1. **Neter** **aah** **utjez** **n-f** **her ren** **f** **Aset** **ur** **hekatyu**
God great raised of-he person name his Isis great words of power

109.2.

109.3. So it has happened that Ra's name has been lifted out of his body. Isis the lady great and mighty of worlds of power

Verse 110.

110.1. **Sheptu** **metu** **pert** **m** **Ra** **arit** **Heru**
Flow poison come out through Ra eye Horus

110.2.

110.3. Has caused to flow the poison, to make it come forth through Ra's body. The eye of Horus

Verse 111.

111.1. **pery** **m** **Neter** **nubau** **n** **ra** **f-y**
come out stepping through the Divinity shining gold of mouth his

111.2.

111.3. also comes forth from the Divinity as shining gold from his mouth.

Verse 112.

112.1. **Nuk** **ari – a** **nuk A** **hau** **er** **maay** **her** **ta**
I done - I I am Divinity come down asto bring on earth

112.2.

112.3. I have done this, it was me. I am the divinity who is the cause of the bringing out of the poison and making it fall down on the ground

Verse 113.

	er	metu	sekhemu	maky	utjez	n	Neter
113.1.							
113.2.		the poison	Life force powers	protection	raised	from	Divinity

113.3. The poison has fallen under the protective vital life forces. Has been lifted up from the Divinity

SECTION: 17-[Verse 114] SHEDY OF NEHAST NEFERHETEP (RESTING IN THE DIVINE ABODE-THRONE OF RA) ASET RESTORES RA TO HEALTH WITH SPECIAL WORDS OF POWER TO HEAL THE MIND AND SOUL HURT BY THE DELUSIONS OF LIFE AND THEREBY ALLOWS CREATION TO REVERT BACK TO ITS ILLUSORY FORM AND RA RETURNS TO CREATING, SUSTAINING, AND CONCLUDING THE DAYS, AND YEARS AS BEFORE

Verse 114.
114.1. *aah   ren   Neter   f   Ra   ankh - f   metut   mer*
114.2. great name divine   his   Ra   live   - he   poison   die.
114.3. The great Divine name his own.   May Ra live and may the poison die. Having achieved the goal of life, the fruit of her dispassion, detachment and concentration on his form, function and nature, the one pointed sacred serpent discipline had served its purpose and now the world was no longer a source of delusion since her existence is now like that of Ra, the magician is not deluded by his own magic. So Ra, the Creation, can continue without deluding her.

Verse 115.
115.1. *tjst   men   a   mes   n   ment*
115.2. reciprocally.   Bound firm person child   of   certain woman
115.3. and conversely.   There is a firm binding trust now between a certain child of a certain woman so

Verse 116.
116.1. *ankh - f   metut   mer   djed   n   Aset   ur*
116.2. life   - he   poison   die.   Speech   of   Isis   great
116.3. that for that child also when the time comes, may the poison die too. These words are by Isis, the great

Mysteries of Isis and Ra

SECTION: 18-[Verse 117] ASET PROVIDES INSTRUCTIONS FOR ANYONE WISHING TO FOLLOW THIS PATH BY A RITUAL THAT INCLUDES: UTTERING THE WORDS OF POWER SHE USED, WITH THE INTENT, FEELING, RELENTLESS INTENSITY SHE APPLIED-ALL TO BE DONE IN FRONG OF SPECIAL IMAGES

Verse 117.

117.1. Henut   neteru   rech   Ra   m   ren   f   djezef

117.2. Mistress   gods & goddesses,   knower   Ra   in   name   his   his own

117.3. Mistress of the gods and goddesses, she who is the knower of Ra's own Divine name!

Verse 118.

118.1. Djed medu   her   tu   n   Temu   hena   Heru   hekenu

118.2. Speak words   upon   image   of   Temu, the finisher   with   Horus   the singer/proclaimer

118.3. She instructs that these words, of this teaching, are to be spoken over an image of the god Temu along with an image of Horus the proclaimer and

Verse 119.

119.1. repyt   Aset   tut   Heru

119.2. image exalted   Isis   image   Horus

119.3. also over an image of the glorious and extolled goddess isis together with an image of Horus.

SCRIPTURE CONCLUDES - HTP

GLOSS ON THE VERSES: Dramatic Reading and Mystic Interpretation of Selected Verses of the Scripture of Aset and Ra

TRANSCRIPT OF THE PRESENTATION OF THE SELECTED VERSES OF THE SCRIPTURE OF ASET AND RA AT THE 2015 NETERIAN CONFERENCE

Note: for the verses not covered in this overview see the course Teachings of the Temple of Aset –www.EgyptianMysterySchool.org

Section 1

I, Muata Ashby have divided the translated text into sections for easier understanding of the phases of the spiritual teaching and spiritual evolution that are being discussed. This division into sections was not done in ancient times, or it would have been done independently by the priests and priestesses during their teaching processes; I assigned these sections, and they are not arbitrarily setup because there are special sections that denote special teachings that are occurring throughout. There are about 19 sections and we are now dealing with Section #1.

In **Verse 1** we were introduced to a special Divinity, there are two similar sounding words, "Ra" is given to Ra the Divinity but it is also to ra or rau, meaning words and this can mean words, it can mean chapters, and it can mean a book of teachings. [As in "Rau nu Pert M Heru" ("Chapters of becoming light").] Rau is words or the chapters of coming forth. So we are introduced to the idea that this teaching is about some special "Dual Divinity", this Divinity is dual in some way, shape or form and maker of Heaven and Earth, the Pet (heavens) and Ta (earth) as well as the "Mau n Ankh chet," the Fire of Life, the Breath of Life. So right at the outset of the teaching you are being told what the scripture is all about. But we're not being told exactly who that divinity is yet but you're introduced to something atypical since most divinities are not dual at least in the context that is being discussed here as we will see.

In verse 1 we are also told that the "Creator" being is also a "maker" or "doer/actor" that in the next verses essentially brought all inanimate and animate things including gods and goddesses, into being. In the Anunian Creation Scripture (see excerpt below) it says the same things as in the present Aset and Ra scripture, but goes a step further and explains that Ra created these things out of the Nun and himself, (which are the same thing actually).[35] This wisdom is certainly part of the Anunian Theology so Aset as a human woman would have studied it along with all other teachings that led her to seek for the divine name of Ra. This is momentous because it is a piece of wisdom that is monumental in scope as it means that if Ra actually is manifesting as the Creation which he brought forth, then it means that when perceiving the physical world and universe we are looking at an illusion due to egoistic living and overproduction of worldly

---

[35] This scripture translation is available in the book *Egyptian Book of the Dead Hieroglyph Translations* by Dr. Muata Ashby.

aryu (unconscious impressions) that have subsumed the original spiritual vision of pure spirit through perceptions using mind and senses exclusively and not using intuitional capacities with which to perceive reality.. This is because we are seeing individual apparently separate objects and do not perceive the underlying nature of objects in Creation, which is one and the same: Ra. So if we perceive the world of time and space as a universe filled with separate and distinct objects with limited lifespans and distinct locations existing in time and space, and we do not perceive that all that is actually Ra, then we have fallen under the delusion of spiritual ignorance. On the other hand knowing this wisdom intellectually, even while not being able to realize its full meaning in fact, and being able to accept it allows dispassion to grow in the mind since there really is nothing in the universe to go after since all is composed of the same essence. Therefore, it is the essence that is to be sought after and if it were sought after exclusively and turning away from the idea that Creation is something other than Spirit manifesting as matter, then this discipline leads to the high achievement of Aset, as a human woman. Based on the understanding of this wisdom, that leads to her relentless and successful practice of motionlessness and serpent power mysticism to pierce through the veil of illusion that is Creation to realize the essence of Creation which as we will see transcends even Ra as a Creator and leads Aset to discover that essence and become one with it and in so doing she realizes herself not just as a human being or a goddess but as the transcendental essence beyond time and space.

Figure 17: Verses 8-10 of the Ancient Egyptian Anunian Creation Scripture

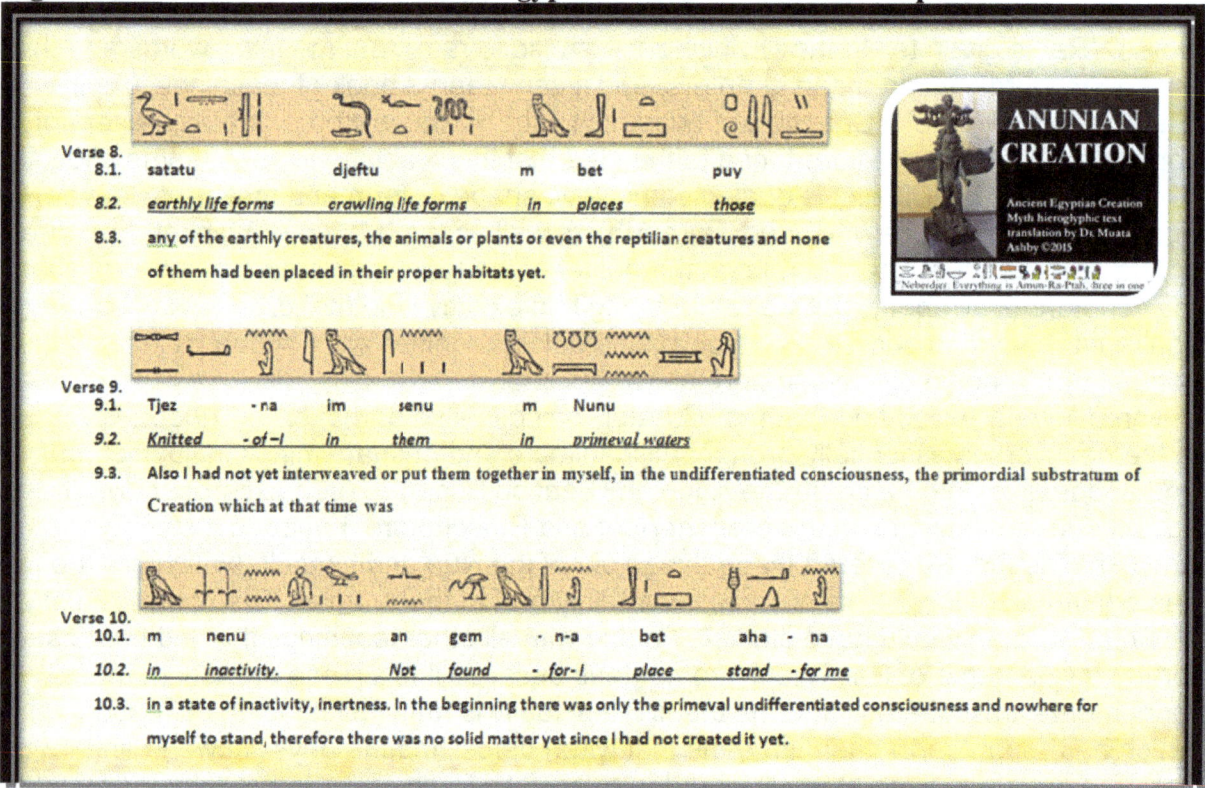

Now in **Verse 3** we have *"Neteru remteju autu menmenu djedftu"* -"Creator of the Gods and Goddesses of men and women and all four legged creatures, cattle, animals of the farm and all forms of reptiles that crawl the earth" So this is the Creator of heaven and earth as well as creator of people and of animals, and now we are differentiating the kinds of animals, so in case you were wondering what those animals are, it is telling you. There are different broad categories of creatures including crawling things, animals running wild, as well as animals that are on the farm, you know the ones that are considered cattle, etc.

Verse 4 - *"apedu remu suten remteju neteru m"* - "flying creatures and creatures of the sea as well. This God is a King over people and also of gods and goddesses…"

Verse 5 - *"cheru ua hentyu er renpetu asha renu"* - "In a form of oneness" so we're kind of being given an allusion to this peculiarity that is being discussed; in Verse 1 we're told this God is a God of Duality and now we're being told something a little different. "In a form of oneness hereby it experiences periods of 120 years as though they are one year, who has many names which are"

Verse 6 - *"an rech pefy. An rech pefy neteru!"* -"whose names are not known. This means names not known even to the Gods and Goddesses!"
Backing up a little bit to Verse 5, we have - a form of oneness whereby it experiences periods of 120 years; so we are being told that this Divinity experiences in a different dimension, a different time and space reality than what humans experience. So for this Divinity that we're being told about, we haven't been told who it is yet, but we are being told about it, that when they experience one year it is as if we experience 120 years. So they're in a different time and space dimension or matrix some would call it. The other importance of Verse 6, as well, is that this Divinity is Dual and apparently it is also Non-Dual because we are being told in Verse 5 that it is also operating in a kind of a oneness and that its essence is not even known by the Gods and Goddesses. So we are being told here now there is a secret, some Shetaut as in Shetaut Neter, some hidden wisdom some hidden understanding here. Not even the Gods and Goddesses know about this, they are not even aware. As has been foreshadowed already, think about what this means so far. That we have a Divinity that is somehow dual and somehow non-dual at the same time and also it is obvious we can take the implication that the non-dual aspect of this Duality is secret even to the Gods and Goddesses. Therefore, it is subtler than the plane of gods and goddesses, which is Creation itself, and time and space. That is what the scripture is about and that is what Aset is seeking. So she is seeking something that not even the Gods and Goddesses know about. That is what I'm getting at, so this is going to allude to why later on she doesn't choose the Gods and Goddesses path. So keep that in mind. So we have something called "Neter Neterty" in Verse 1, a Dual Divinity, and now in Verse 5 we are to understand that it operates in "Kheru Ua", a form of Oneness that is in a different dimension and the knowledge of this is not known to even the Gods and Goddesses.

Section 2 - Listening to the Teachings Part 2 - Understanding the Trouble of Life, Dispassion, Detachment, and Choice of Life Path

Verse 7 - *"Astu Aset m zet saa n"* - "Look here comes Isis in the form of a physical human woman who is also expert on the subject of..."
In Verse 7 we are being told, and this is unmistakable due to the way the text is constructed, the manner in which the grammar is arranged, we are being told that this is a physical, human person in case you had any doubts or any kind of quandaries about the issue and specifically one of the main reasons is so you can know that you, as a human, the reader of this text, so that you can know, in no uncertain terms, that what is being told here, in this scripture, is for human beings and is attainable by human beings. Again, just in case you had any doubts. Because you might want to say, "Oh this is about Goddess Aset and she did this and it's all mythic and it's all metaphorical, for gods and goddesses, and it's all, you know, way up there and us humans can't do all that stuff, etc." A lot of people like to fall back on those conclusions based on ignorant notions or willful misunderstanding based on a desire not to follow such teachings and thereby have an excuse to discount them and thereby not have to do them. They use that as their out, excuses to not adopt a higher teaching and path of life and instead stay wallowing in the mediocrity of life. "Oh that's too much for me, only some higher being can attain that; I'm just human, I'm only human." Or "I'm doing the best I can, leave me alone." Some people need to cope that way otherwise they will have a nervous breakdown, which is understandable, which is ok. For those who have a different perspective, maturity and advancing ethical conscience and have a more balanced, purified personality and also a higher will capacity, they have a different path to follow and that is what the scripture is written for, for those personalities and not for the ones who want to discount it and throw it out and continue living egoistic lives. There are three main things in these verses, first of all, that she is human; second of all, the last part of Verse 7 which says that she is "Saa n" and then "djedu" that's where this sentence actually ends. Meaning that she has knowledge of words and as we said before her words are words-Ra-Chapters-Teachings. So she is an expert in words, particularly in speech, so she is a philosopher, knowing the philosophy of knowledge. Knowledge about what though? Knowledge of worldly disciplines, knowledge of science, knowledge healing, she is kind of like an Imhotep character, a Renaissance person. They have several languages they know, several academic degrees, several disciplines that they are good at and she is that type of personality; everyone has that capacity to do that except to the extent of the level of their Aryu (sum total of past experiences lodged in the unconscious that colors the mind and causes a person to think, feel, desire and act in certain ways and not in others) that is limiting them. Then the next important teaching that occurred in the verse is the last part where it starts to say:

Verse 8 - and in Verse 9: *"djedu kha-k ab z er hehu m"* - we are going to see what that is about. Basically, it says she is knowledgeable in the writings of the teachings *"writings about worldly subjects. With all that understanding about worldly affairs, her heart was* *disappointed, even sick, so she was disgusted in her heart about the millions of manifestations called"*

Verse 9 - *"renteju setep res hehu m neteru apt - set"* - So she is disgusted about the deluded, unfulfilling human existence. All human existence that is not dedicated to the higher purpose of discovering the nature of self is wasteful and detestable. If you are a worldly person you are what she is disgusted about. So she is disgusted *"of human beings, their activities, they're futile pursuits."* After evaluating the prospect of living life as an ordinary human being she became dispassionate and disillusioned about that; next she considered the options of millions of Gods and Goddesses as better; But before we go there, there is more to understand about the issue of *"Khak -ab"*. Khak -ab means "sick at heart" or: disgusted" and thus dispassionate, it means "detached" and this is a foundation for the spiritual teachings. If you don't have that feature in the personality you can do all your other spiritual disciplines but you will be caught up in the world again later on. You can be very well versed in the philosophy, you can be coming to classes and even be a teacher of yoga, etc. and then, all of a sudden, you get caught up in some worldly situation. That is because you haven't had the full "Khak ab" attainment; your heart has to be fully disillusioned about the world it cannot be just disappointed. As Seba Dja was saying earlier, in her lecture, being disappointed you may be like Elizabeth Taylor, and end up with the 10th husband or like Halle Berry, maybe the next one will be the one, instead of fixing the problem which is internal. It is the problem of feeling and experiencing life as a fragmented being in need of seeking something to find wholeness. This is due to egoism and egoism is due to aryu; egoism causes you to think you are a separate and limited and weak individual so you need to latch on to other people and objects to feel yourself fulfilled and whole but that never happens since the flaw is within you and nothing from the outside world can fulfil that need since it is illusory. In reality, you are whole and you can regain that wholeness if you find the secret knowledge about this Neter Neterty divine essence. That is what Aset is seeking. The discovery of that resolves the problem of desiring and trying to be fulfilled by external aspects of life which can never bring fulfillment or abiding satisfaction.

Figure 18: (on following page) From the book of Coming Forth By Day-Hymn to Asar

The Hymn to Asar (PMH & Asarian Resurrection Myth)
Perseverance & being Relentless

Aset   Akht   anetj   sent–s   hehit   su   antet   begag   kabert   ta
Isis   shining spirit protector brother hers seeking he   not resting around the earth planet
djed   kha-k   ab   ser   hehu m remtj   setep res
words (of power) repudiating heart (hers) millions of men and women, choosing (instead)
  not faltering
  not weary
  not helpless
  not discouraged
  not dissuaded

pen   m   hay   an   chen   nez   an   gemtu   s   su
this   form   lamentations   not alighting   did she not finding   she he
this one, and making utterances of divine words of caring for the lost one to be found and Returned to glory, she did not even stop to take a rest as long has he was not found!!!

This is a Bonus slide related to the teaching of Aset and Ra. One part was presented at last year's conference and this is pretty much the same the text from the Asarian Resurrection where it says, *"Aset Aket anteg sent-s hehit su antet begag kabert ta"* - *"Isis shining spirit protector brother hers seeking he not resting around the earth, planet".* Remember from the Asarian Resurrection epic, when Asar was killed by Set and his body was thrown in the Nile River and his body went floating away. Aset found out about it and then she went searching all over the world. So the text I gave last year gave you the "Antet Begag" teaching where she won't rest while she is looking, searching, not faltering, not wearying, not helpless, not discouraged, not dissuaded. The new part is this script on the bottom which follows is the next sentence: *"pen m hey an chen nez an gemtu s su"* - "this form lamentations not alighting did she not finding she he" that was the direct translation. *"this one and making utterances of divine words of caring for the lost one to be found and returned to glory she did not even stop to take a rest as long as he was not found."* So Antet Begag implies the not being discouraged, and being relentless. However the scripture adds the second sentence in case you didn't understand the emphasis of this issue so it gives you Antet Begag which means not relenting. It means you don't give up, it means you don't become disheartened and say, "Oh this is too hard, I'll never reach this goal, let me just forget it, I'll never get it, let me just stay at home and just let it be and live my life."

But in the next sentence it says, "an chen" - not alighting. Alighting is when a bird stops its flying and perches itself on a branch and takes a little rest and then keeps on going. So it's saying, metaphorically, is that you can't even do that. So it means that you don't take a break, and that you are not going to be coming to learn this teaching and say, "Oh that was really good, I did all my postures this week and I studied the scripture, I saw the lecture with Sebai Maa online, so it is Friday night I'm going to party with my friends and go drinking and dancing, driving out to Vegas and having whatever fun we want and when we come back on Monday we'll be back to the teaching." That's an extreme example but you know when you go to a movie or you pass on vegetarianism and say, "I've been doing that for the last month I can have a little hamburger, it's not going to hurt, a little steak, it's no problem." So it means you should not stop to take a break from the spiritual program of life, no break from the movement towards the spiritual goal. You should not take this literally, that you shouldn't be sitting, you should always be standing, or that if you're tired you can't sit down or take a nap or sleep at night. It means that your perspective has to be constant and growing with intensity. But it cannot be out of balance or with undue stress. An airplane requires the balance of two wings to move up whether the angle of movement is gentle or steep.

===============SPECIAL NOTE=================
So these are important keys of Aset mythic wisdom and mystical philosophy: 1-*Khak-ab* [dispassion/detachment/disillusionment with the world], 2-*antet begag* [relentless effort to study and practice and transform the personality by understanding and seeking the Divine] and 3-*an chen* [not stopping the effort towards the Divine]. If these keys were to be studied and practiced in earnest and with proper guidance, they lead to the coveted goal of the teachings.
==================================

Verse 10 - *"hehu m akhu shepsu an khemn set m pet"* - So she was disgusted about ordinary people with worldly conscience and spiritual ignorance. She was disgusted with those people out there who are running after the world in time and space trying to be happy by getting a new car or by getting money, or by fame or love affairs, watching soap operas, and this one screws over another and falls in love with the next one or having sex indiscriminately, or drugs and alcohol that distort perceptions, or watching TV or other mindless entertainments and not thinking about the higher aspects of life. The point is that she was disgusted with them and thought, "maybe I should go after the Gods and Goddesses instead of human life because that is supposed to be a better way of life right?"

The idea here is that after living life of as a human being, and experiencing the disappointments and frustrations that never end, eventually you will be led to this, lead to a desire for a higher way of life, maybe it might take a few million lifetimes. If you are a God and Goddess, they live on a different time dimension and maybe it might take them a few thousand generations of incarnations, so wouldn't that be ok with you.

Or maybe there is a better alternative. Better than the people - *remteju* - in Verse 9; better than the *Neteru*, the Gods, and Goddesses. The Neteru are better but even they did not know the secret of Neter Neterty. What about the *Akhu Shepsu, the enlightened noble personalities*? So s
he then considered what about the millions of enlightened sages and saints? What if instead of being an ordinary mortal woman or a goddess she instead were to become like them? Not being spiritually ignorant and existing in the heavenly plane, she is talking about here not just having higher consciousness here on the Earth plane, the *Ta* plane, she is talking about *Pet*, the heavenly plane also. So she is talking about achieving the Dual Consciousness. About the term "Akhu Shepsu", Shepsu is a term for a venerated ancestor or a wise person; it can also mean a sage type of personality. If you put *Akh* before it, it means spiritual and Akh is the highest level of spiritual consciousness that everyone has but not everyone is aware of. But those who are Akh Sheps, they are venerated because they have become enlightened. The Akh by itself also means enlightenment. It means being of light, a shining spirit. So she thought I'm doing all this effort so why not go for that instead, go for that higher road, and go all the way?

Verse 11 - *"ta mi Ra ari gert ta"* And not being of the earth plane (from Verse 10) and then there is another thought that comes in because she has been, as you are going to see later, practicing the Hymn to Ra and she had studied the Anunian Creation myth and that has already given her certain insights that we are going to discuss later, as a kind of back story to this. But for now she is saying, "I'm rejecting the path of ordinary people, refusing the path of the Gods and Goddesses, I'm considering the Akhu Shepsu, and they are pretty good, but there is also another way that is even more direct, is it possible for me too?"

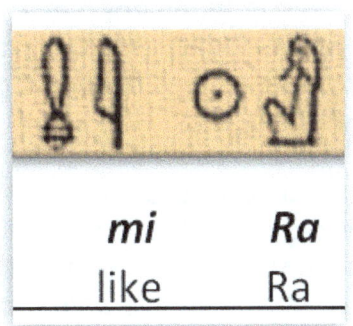

Section of Verse 11

Let me read the verse first, *"but in effect to be like Ra? That is to become Divine as He, a Divinity as He by appropriating for myself the Divine knowledge that He has and then on earth even while alive I could be a"*. We will see what that means in Verse 12. This term here, this "mi" is a kind of metaphorical statement. It doesn't mean that she wants to become Ra, it is becoming like Ra which means becoming like what Ra is. So the question then is it possible to bypass the other paths, going straight to the Divine Self? Going straight to heaven, going straight to The Source of transcendental consciousness and Supreme Existence?

It is a good idea but most people are not ready for it; even those who say they are, who think they are, they are not ready for it, that's really the truth of the matter. You have to understand what it is or ready yourself to be able to do this serious road. We will talk about this a little more later. I kind of alluded to this earlier; there are some people who have come to Shetaut Neter or Vedanta Philosophy, or the Tao or any other higher teachings and they are very enthusiastic, very gung-ho let's call it and they have some of these aspects of khak-ab, antet begag and an chen, being dispassionate, not relenting and not stopping but then somehow the aryu is not cleansed enough and the negative side, the Setian side comes up and somehow thwarts the movement of the soul and that is an important aspect of the story of the Asarian Resurrection.

This is an important aspect of the teaching. When we come to Verse 8, this is giving the indication that Aset, as a woman, had listened to the teaching previously and she is arriving here, to the study of this teaching and its experiences as a qualified aspirant, ready to go. She has already dealt with the psychological issues that plague most of humanity, and she is through with seeking happiness or fulfilment from the world; she is of resolute mind: "I'm here for this teaching and that's it." She is not going to be like those aspirants who attend classes and keep on reincarnating and becoming yoga practitioners but never progressing to the finish line, coming to the world again and again and keep learning but not achieving steadiness and strong dispassion; those are like the takeoff of a rocket that never attains escape velocity and will fall back to earth. This is not that kind of scripture. This teaching of Aset and Ra scripture is about when you're ready to achieve the fullness of dispassion, detachment, and become proficient in the lower mystery practices (worldly knowledge) so then now you are ready to move up to take the next steps into the higher mysteries (knowledge of Spirit). That is an important thing to understand. That is one of the things that makes this scripture special because in this term *Khak-ab*, therein lies a vast teaching of letting go of the world, a teaching of dispassion and detachment that allows the soul to take off and escape the pull of the gravity of egoism and its encircling moons of anger, hatred, fear, desire and delusions. In the next verses, she is talking about the choices of human beings, or Gods and Goddesses or Akhu Shepsu.

The question is how to gauge where one is on the spiritual path? It is done by being quiet and balanced (Maat) enough to be able to be sensitive to one's own thoughts and feelings, if you are not sensitive then you can't really have Saa. Saa is knowledge and feeling of the truth. If you have worldly aryu (content of unconscious mind) then the saa (intellectual and feeling capacity) will be atrophied, leading to distorted, warped ways of feeling about and thinking and conclusions about issues in life. If you are partial to desires they will keep on coming up and urging the pursuit of them and if they are strong enough they will compel you to an action against your will. If you have strong enough will to say, "stop eating sugar, stop eating meat" but you still have desires coming up and every time you see it you wish you could even though you resist it that means that it is still there. It has to be dealt with, it has to be neutralized. It can come up and undermine your positive efforts; it's like quicksand of negative feelings and warped intellectual support of those, and one day you can be bingeing on a whole gallon of ice cream and not know what happened.

Verse 12 - We come in from Verse 11 "and then on earth even while alive I could be a Goddess." So now she is talking about becoming a goddess and what she means by becoming a goddess is being like Ra. Understand what that means, in the Henotheistic conception we have a Supreme Being and you have several Gods and Goddesses that emanate from that One God, and that is Henotheism. She is not talking about being a God or Goddess like an emanation but rather she is talking about being one with the top, on the top level, the source. You have to shift your thinking to understand that Ra is a level of Divinity. There's not just one Ra so anybody could attain that and be like Ra in other words you can attain that level of consciousness.

Section 3 – LADY ASET'S EARLY REFLECTIONS, MEDITATIONS, AND CONCLUSIONS

Aset had wisdom philosophical reflections. She listened to the teachings, now she is reflecting on the choices she can make. First of all another point I wanted to make. This teaching of Aset is what we call a Wisdom Path. In the Wisdom Path, you do practice meditation. In the Wisdom Path, there are three steps, listening, reflection and meditation. The whole thing (all three steps) is a meditation discipline, but the last step, that we would call a formal aspect. These other aspects, the listening, and the reflection are informal aspects of meditation. But it is all meditative process. As you've probably discerned by now all of this process is about building a Taffy Shepsy, that is, creating of yourself a one-pointed serpent power movement towards the Divine. All your listening work to the teaching in trying to understand, all your reflecting and being dispassionate and how you deal with that in day to day life is so you can create that process? It is that you are cleansing your unconscious mind, your Ab, cleansing it of the negative Aryu. That is actually allowing the energy that is locked up in that negative Aryu to be released and the goes into your Arat Sekhem, your Serpent Power and that is the Taffy Shepsy that is being built. So even without thinking about Serpent Power or doing anything special you are building the Serpent Power even through this discipline. So the listening and reflection, those are steps 1 and 2 of the meditation process and what we call meditation at the end that is the full one-pointedness of the Taffy Shepsy. When all the thoughts are coming into a focus and you don't have disparaging thoughts plaguing you and haunting you, this desire or that desire or that's troubling me, or this person, or the war over there, or everything. And when there is a cessation of movement, then all that energy can come to a focus and that is what is called the Taffy Shepsy. From a mythological standpoint, yes there is a crawling creature that goes around and wiggles and gets quiet in the sky on the path of the sun god, etc. That is metaphoric language, figurative language referring to what is happening to the serpent power in the body and mind of a human being as it raises and gets closer to the paraclete[36] God manifestation to break through the illusion of Creation so that the soul may discover the truth of existence. From a mystic standpoint, you are the Taffy Shepsy that you are transforming yourself into. That is the difference between myth, ritual, and mysticism. The people outside of the Temple, the masses, had been told the mythic truth about the teaching, its exoteric aspects, but not the mystic esoteric insights about it; yes she created this serpent and it was wiggling around in the sky and it bit Ra. But for initiates, you are being told the real deal. Why? Because you have applied yourself, you have knocked on the door of the Temple, and people from the Temple know that you are serious. Unlike people who are not here in the temple or studying this text with proper guidance, but you are here. So you get to be introduced to the teaching.

---

[36] In religious studies the concept of "Paraclete" refers to an "an advocate or intercessor" so in this context mythically Ra is the High God of the Henothistic (supreme god manifesting as several lesser divinities) system of gods and goddesses of Anunian Religious tradition of Ancient Egypt. However, this scripture is alluding to an intercessor role.

So Verse 12, she wants to know is it possible at this point? She is asking the question at this point. She's going through the Akhu Shepsu and the Neteru, the Remteju, can I go directly and discover and be a Goddess like Ra? Then she started doing some deeper reflection and it says, (Verse 12) "ka set m ab set er chen rech" - "Aset thought deeply about the issue (started concentrating and bringing her mind to think about these issues) then she began to think more deeply." So the term *Ka* here represents reflection, which is a mental act of cognition and thought/concept comparison. Then it says, "that she brought those reflections into her heart." At this point, she has turned her attention away from the world and its sense perceptions and inwards towards her deeper mental processes, her subconscious, and unconscious. So she is seriously meditating now on this issue. This level of meditation is still in the lower mind; it is not the level of meditation that occurs when the Taffy Shepsy is complete. This current level is still moving towards that completion stage. When it is complete then it can be piercing through the illusion. So we are not at that stage yet. So she is meditating deeply in her heart as to the wisdom.

Verse 13 - about the name Divine - *"Ren Neter shepsy"* - "the Divine name of Ra, the exalted name, the saintly, virtuous, spiritual name of Ra?" She is realizing and understanding, from her studies, that if she were able to attain the true name of Ra then that would be her pathway to attain Goddess-hood; to be like Ra, because when you have the name of something you have the essence of that something and the essence of Ra is the goal. In a wider sense, this means that all the names that you know that are time and space based; they are all based on ignorance. You don't know anything about the deeper nature of reality if all you know is a descriptive name of an object. That descriptive name tells you nothing about the essence of the object. The spiritual name we are looking for is that deeper essence and not the surface description.

Even the essence of what these cells, the energy of the body, the clothing that you are looking at, etc., none of that is a reality but just a description of an appearance. You don't know exactly what the deeper reality is; if you knew what the reality was then you would have the true knowledge of what that is. An electron-microscope would not even tell you. So all the things that we name, this is a house, this is a computer, this is a chair, this is a pair of pants, this is clothes, this is a shirt, this is a person, this is a dog, that is a cat, this is this, that is that, etc., none of those things are realities; those are all mental conventions based on superficial sense perceptions and limited intellectual capacity. Those are practical realities that the mind and society have accepted for practical reasons, but which are wrong from an absolute truth standpoint.

That acceptance of those as realities is what is causing you to have the desires and the repudiations of life that provoke mental agitations and push you towards things or that push you away from things, and causes fluctuations in your mind that contribute to forming a curtain that shields your awareness from the higher reality. If you were really able to tap into that higher reality, you would realize that all this is an illusion. That is the teaching that Aset is trying to learn. It is being alluded to in this scripture and now she is taking the next step in reading into it as we are going to see. This is what the clear thinking and lucid reasoning is there for and these are the conclusions that are coming up because of it.

============== Questions and Answers ================

Question to Dr. Ashby:

Yes, so you are navigating along the path that consciousness is the only reality in everything that we see and experience is a projection of that consciousness?

Sebai Maa - From a relative standpoint your question is correct but even the idea of consciousness is a concept and is not real. Anything that you conceive of in your mind, think about in your mind is based on a conditioned reality that you have accepted that is not true.

Questioner: Concept another concept.

Sebai Maa - Because your mind is limited and because the world is changing constantly you can never put your finger on the reality. Except if you were to follow this path, then you would have a chance to discover the reality by going beyond mind and the changeable time and space and that's what we're talking about. Then having done that, then you come back to this time and space reality and you hang out.

Questioner - So Sebai you are talking beyond what is said to be pure consciousness which is another label also or concept?

Sebai Maa - Right, concepts are used to point to the higher truth; they are not the higher truth itself so in the end they are let go once they serve their philosophical purpose. If we turn off all the lights in the room, you are not blind but you cannot see and then we close the windows and doors and we somehow put you in a room and you don't know where the doors are, you don't know where the windows are but somebody says on a loudspeaker, "Get out, you have to get out of this room now." What is going to happen? You're going to be groping, you are going to be bumping into each other. You say, "Oh this person is in my way and I have to have a war against you so I can get out of here etc." But what if somebody wise, even in the darkness of the dark room were to say, "Hey I'm touching something here and this is a door, follow my voice. Follow the path that I'm telling you." So even within the darkness, there is a kind of path to the light, even though the path part of the illusory room yet it leads to freedom from the illusion. Though you are not blind to the higher self you cannot see it and need guidance to lead yourself to it. So you can't get caught into that everything is illusion because you will throw everything out, the baby with the bathwater, so to speak; that is Nihilism which doesn't work, from a practical standpoint-unless mind is completely ready to let go of the practical reality and embrace the essence of being that lies beyond mind and time and space. It is a philosophical and psycho-mystic truth that is to be understood and experienced. Yet the philosophical description is necessary to point an aspirant in the right direction even though when the destination of the absolute truth is reached it will be different than the philosophy. The philosophy is not wrong but the absolute experience transcends its best tenets. However, those philosophical tenets allow the mind to be made lucid enough so as to be able to intuitively understand even if intellectually the thoughts lead to impasses. This affords the capacity to move forward on the spiritual path beyond ego and mind and the capacity to step into, as we will see, a higher plane of existence that transcends human existence.

Question- So if everything in our mind is an illusion, everything that we can think of is an illusion how is it that what we think manifests? What we think we create from illusion also?

Sebai Maa - Because you have spark of spirit and you can control a certain measure of the Chet n Ankh and the Nafu n Ankh, the Fire of Life, and Breath of Life; with a portion of these you can manifest to a limited degree. You have enough spirit and power to create a dream world, when you sleep, and everything in it is made up of your mind sustained by the consciousness of your soul, which is a drop in the ocean of Spirit. In fact, you had enough power that you projected your personality, you projected your body, you have caused it to come into existence, and your parents were the venue, a vehicle for that. You are the one creating your life and you can change your life by changing your aryu through the practice of shedy (Kemetic yoga Egyptian mysteries) disciplines. You may be able to change a lot of things in the world. Some people have more power than others to change things. They may become presidents or they become corporate leaders. Others remain as garbage men or maids, etc., all depending on aryu, which is the filter used by the soul to exist in time and space and partake in the illusory realities created by the mind beset by ignorance as well as the ignorance and delusions of others as well as the unintelligible marvel that is Creation, albeit in a deluded fashion.

Follow-up Question - Now that's also still an illusion is it not?

Sebai Maa - It is all illusion, your internal concepts, and desires as well as that of others as well as your limited perceptions of the world and human existence, all illusory. You can be the most powerful person, you can be an emperor and it is still and illusion. But you need a certain level of freedom, space and sanity and wherewithal to be able to follow the teaching also. You can't be just a poor person on the street, suffering or sick you have to have some level of wherewithal to practice the teaching. Also, being too involved with the world with lots of money and power can be as distracting as being poor and troubled.

===========END QUESTIONS AND ANSWERS============

Verse 13 - So this name, this *Ren*, is *Neter Shepsy* or sanctified, holy divinity name as we said Sheps means sanctified, it means virtuous, exalted.

Figure 19: Ancient Egyptian Image of the three forms of Ra: Ra-Khepri (Khepera), Ra-Herakhty and Ra-Tem

Verse 16 - *"Aaut netery nenu n-f ra f"* - "The Divine one of the two horizons had become old and had to leave his perches and head for the western horizon of heaven. As he moved along shuffling with his walking stick, he started drooling from his mouth." So Ra has the three stages. He is Khepera in the morning, he is Ra Herakty, Ra of the Two Horizons in midday, and he is Ra Tem in the evening. But in the evening he gets tired, he gets old, he starts drooling, the spittle starts coming out of the side of his mouth.

Verse 17 - *"satet f nebaut f er Ta"* - So Ra-Tem has got a little spittle coming out at say 3 PM if the sunset is at 6 PM. Then as we get closer to like 5 it starts really coming out. He's looking pretty bad; Really messed up and old. He's not like an 110 yr. old person who can't speak and carry on, be lucid, etc. but he is like losing it, ready to die, which is at sunset, But at sunset Nut eats him and then she revives him and gives birth to him the next day, but that is a different part of the myth of Ra, in the Creation scripture,[37] we are just dealing with the sunset part. In Verse 17 it starts pouring out, it is not just drooling now, and it is pouring out. "old age has struck Ra who at this stage is now called Ra-Tem, his mature mid-day RaHarakty form. It is as if an arrow has pierced his nature and his drool has now turned into fluid pouring out of his body, the emanations which are dropping on the earth below as he courses through the sky towards the end of the day(in the west)." So we are going to talk more about what these emanations are.

---

[37] (of course he does not die because his mother Nut renews him to be reborn the next morning as Khepera the Creator of the new day-but this is in the Creation scripture).

Mysteries of Isis and Ra

SECTION 4: SHEDY OF ACTION AND DEVOTION (EMOTION) TO GOD IN FORM OF RA-TEM; A RITUAL OBSERVANCE IN LATE AFTERNOON, DEVOTIONAL REMEMBRANCE AND MEDITATION, VIEWING RA AND COLLECTING RA'S LIFE FORCE EMANATIONS TO BUILD CONCENTRATION ON RA AND SPIRITUAL STRENGTH FOR ONE-POINTEDNESS OF MIND ON THE FORM, MOVEMENTS AND ACTIONS OF RA AND FINALLY THE ESSENCE OF RA.

I'm giving you an allusion to what the meditation is, it is a movement of devout worship leading to a concentration on Ra's forms, on his movements, his actions and then finally on his essence which transcends his forms, transcends his movements, and his appearances and his symbols.

Verse 18 - *"Pagas n su secher her satyu sek n s Ast"* There is a lot of spittle, a lot falling on faces flooding and collecting to she Isis. "The saliva of Ra Tem was falling voluminously now on the faces of persons, flooding all over the land, exposed to half of the sky knowing its significance Isis collected it for herself." What is going on here is that toward the end of the day you notice that even in the morning or the evening you can stand to be outside, the heat of the sun is not going to cook you, it is not going to burn you, it will just be a little warm. So it is a lot cooler. So it is not something that you would want to do when Ra Herakty is out, when the mid-day sun is out because that will do you in. But at the end of the day because of the position of the sun, the earth and the atmosphere, for several reasons the emanations of Ra are very cool and soothing and you are able to accept more of the emanation, more of the sunshine at that time. As you know when you are eating plants you are actually eating green sunshine. Plants take the sunshine that plants have processed, into chlorophyll and into other nutrients. To some extent also you need to have direct sunlight yourself to form Vitamin D and for other processes. There's a study that I have not verified yet but it is finding that there are some newly discovered receptors in the eyes, beyond the cones and rods that make use of sunlight. You don't have to look at the sun; this is just by being out and basking in the sunlight. It has certain receptors that have a certain effect on your nervous system, that is what this study was finding but I haven't verified it. This is part of that importance of doing morning or evening ritual. But we are talking about the evening ritual right now.

Question - Kind of like in winter where people are (SAD)?

Sebai Maa - Right they get depressed, a lot of people get sad. The Seasonal Affective Disorder (SAD) so a lot of people in northern latitudes have a lot of problems with that. They have a lot of depression. What is going on here in the mythic aspect of the scripture is this saliva, this special cooling, which is an accessible emanation of Ra and it is shining on everybody, on half of the world as you know and Aset noticed this and she started collecting it, started collecting this emanation with intent. As opposed to people who are walking around at the same time but they are going to the store. Another one is going to visit family. Another one is going shopping or to a movie or something else. But some are saying, "wow the sun is out, let me turn my attention to the sun, turn my adorations, let me utter the Hymn to Ra Tem and let me consciously think about Ra Tem and the thoughts of Ra and the energies of Ra within myself." So people can have their attention on horizontal time and space issues or on vertical spiritual issues. That is what Aset is doing she is conscious as opposed unconscious. In saying that this emanation is falling on everybody but Aset noticed that and she started collecting it. We have images such as these of Ra emanating rays in the form of lotuses and it is hitting the face of this initiate who in this aspect is called Aset. Here is Akhenaton and he is collecting the life giving Rays of Aton(Ra) I used to do this kind of thing years ago of putting out glass bottles of purified water, leave it out all day and take it at the end of the day and it is energized with solar energy.

Figure 20: Sunrays of Ra shine on the forehead of Aset

Figure 21: Akhenaton and Nefertiti receiving rays from Aton

Mysteries of Isis and Ra

SECTION 5: SHEDY OF ACTION AND RIGHT RITUAL DISCIPLINE OF WORKING DAY BY DAY GATHERING SPIRITUAL STRENGTH AND STAMINA FASHIONING ONESELF INTO THE SACRED SERPENT FOR ONE POINTED VISION.

Verse 19 - *"M det set hena ta unentu her set qed nez set"* So she was collecting it in her hands, she's collecting the spittle, which is the sun rays, the cooling sun rays which are allowing us to have a kind of deeper access to the spiritual being of Ra, spiritual essence of Ra, that we don't have the rest of the day because we are too busy sheltering from the power of the rays during those times. So she collects the spittle with her hands and with some soil being on her. This is how the text is written and read; it is as if the soil is on her; she is picking it up so that she can take those to herself. But also what is her skin made up of? It is made of the elements of the earth and water. So it is alluding to the idea that she is composed of matter and she is collecting something subtler, the emanations of Ra that enliven the matter. It is saying that those emanations are also falling on her too, on her person so she starts kneading. Kneading is like when you are fashioning silly putty or clay, so she starts working on that, working on her person, on her personality. It says she is collecting what belongs to her. Meaning, she is collecting what is falling on and around her, what she has access to and is meant for her. So she is not depriving us of anything we can be doing the same thing too. Ra's energy is abundant.

Verse 20 - *"m djedfty shepsy ari n set m"* - In this scripture, the Taffy Shepsy is referred to as Djedfty Shepsy. So she is collecting and kneading it or forming it "in the form of a spiritually consecrated serpent making it for/to herself in the form of"

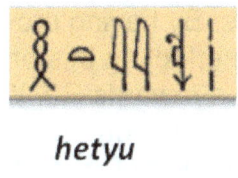

hetyu

harpoon

Verse 21 - *"qaa hetyu an nemu nemu a z"* - "an image of a harpoon having a shaft that ends in one point but (this is the critical point) but the image of that sacred serpent was not moving yet." So she was kneading it, forming, fashioning it into a shape and that is "shepsy" meaning that it is revered, that it is holy. You can concentrate on things that are holy or on things that are criminal and be a crook; one can concentrate on how can I steal something? How is the best way to commit fraud at the bank so people will lose their house and money and so they won't even know it before it's gone and I can get away with it legally? There's lots of smarts there, lots of one-pointedness of mind towards those negative goals there but that is Setian, that's not Shepsy. She is creating a shepsy taffy movement, a shepsy serpentine movement. This is another allusion I want to add to this same issue. It is related to the serpent power as well as what we are talking about, that the Serpent Power can be positive or negative. If you create positive Serpent Power it will move your consciousness upwards. If you create negative it will move downwards. The positive movement is creating higher consciousness; the lower movement is creating other people and worldly situations. That's how people grow legs. You have two legs when you grow up and then you have a baby and now you have four legs; of course if you have another baby now you have six legs, etc. Having lots of legs could be good if you were a caterpillar because then you could move fast but being human this slows you down. Adding other people to your life, such as progeny or other family or friends, etc., is fine for those who are at the level of necessity for human or worldly relationships. If you've moved on beyond those dependencies or needs or if you've had your children, so been there and done that, then you can say "now kha-k ab with that" then good for you, then more power to you, then you've worked through that issue and you are ready to move on. But we're not saying anything bad about people who want to do that, it is just understanding that these are levels of the movement of consciousness through the process of spiritual evolution.

The other important aspect that is being given in Verse 21 is "an nemu nemu". This is another important aspect of the meditation system that I have not talked about yet. The "an nemu nemu" means that you have a serpent that is motionless, that is not moving and this is an important aspect of the meditation system. Becoming introspective and more considered in one's motions facilitates placing the mind in a meditative framework. Therefore, pulling back from unnecessary agitating activities and or approaching these in a less agitated manner is part of the discipline of the Temple of Aset. Therefore, motion of all kinds is to be considered carefully before engaging in such. Motion is the key to Creation and therefore the opposite of motion, motionlessness, is a key to unraveling the mysteries of Creation because it allows one-pointedness of mind to be achieved. When you come to a point, to one-pointedness of mind, there's not movement anymore. There's no physical movement, and there's no mental movement. You can have no mental movement two ways. By having movement in one direction, or having no movement at all. It has the same effect. In this one we are discussing movement as in one direction, that is, concentration towards Ra. What this is alluding to is that you should not have movement or variation in your mind. Like at one moment you are thinking, "oh look at the wonderful image of Ra, and this is so great and look at the colors, worshippers, me sitting here in front of the image, etc., etc." Your next thought is, "oh what am I having for dinner?" "Oh, what is going to be on TV tonight?" "Oh, look at Ra again." "Oh I forgot to call my mother; I forgot to pick something up at the store; oh, Ra again." This is disjointed mental movement, not one pointed movement. This is the kind of mental movement that causes variations in the mind, fluctuations and drainage of mental power as well as distraction and reversion back to the ego self, like a house of mirrors where your vision is fragmented into various images of the ego personality, yourself. Remember the teaching of the wisdom texts (see below), saying that the cause of your incarnation is the back and forth of the mind, the love and the hate movement in the mind. If you stop hating things, stop loving things, your mind starts settling down and you'd be able to have peace, hetep and one-pointedness. If you keep on trying to fix the world or think that the world is real and you have to live in it and do the things that people are doing and pursue those things in order to be fulfilled or happy, that ignorant path of life is going to keep you engaged, it's going to keep you caught, constantly agitated, disturbed and with a warped mind that is not fit for advancing in the teaching of the mysteries. That is not Kha-k Ab it is the opposite. So "an nemu nemu" –

we have to stop the constant movement and let go of the world and let it do its thing. One final point here is that in the beginning motionlessness takes effort; so it can be hard to sit still and even harder to concentrate the mind and let it stay motionless. When there is success in this practice, meaning that the motionlessness becomes spontaneous and the object of concentration itself becomes the most attractive magnetic power drawing attention, as if it were a black hole that sucks in all matter and even light, and since mind is composed of subtle matter it also gets drawn towards the object and the objective of the teaching and thus the practice becomes self sustaining and through a process of positive feedback loops (collection and accumulation of the energy, production of new concentration and hetep (non-dual) aryu) it becomes more powerful until it can overwhelm the power of Ra (illusoriness of Creation over the mind).

Figure 22: Review-PMH Chap 30 -Heart as Cause of Incarnation

PertemHeru Chap. 30A
The Heart as Cause of Incarnation
Ma'at as the path of Enlightenment

Ab – a n mut-a   zep sen hatyab– a n   un – a   dep   ta
Heart mine mother mine twice. heart mine cause of existing on earth.

m aha   er a   m **meteru**   rem   neb   chetu
Manner rising not obstructing me as witness in presence lord judgment balance

m djed   er – a   iu   ari n – f   zet   er   **un**   Ma'at
Manner speaking about me it is worked he against the absolute right & truth, order, justice.
existence
ever-presence
reality
being
continuation

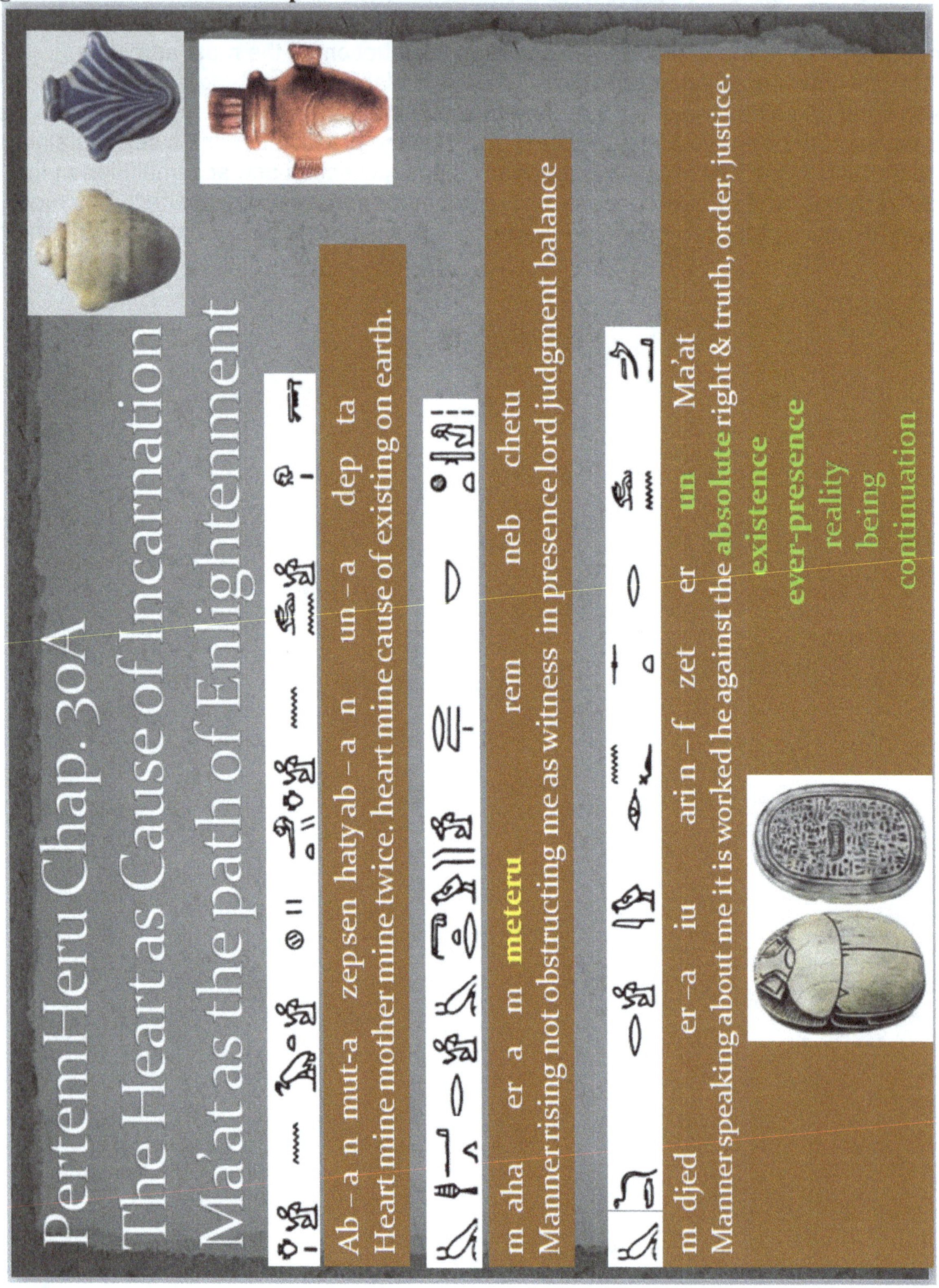

Verse 27 - *"seft seft f mi Ra neb unchu set"* - "Striding along as usual, as he did every day along the same path, he was bitten by means of a

Verse 28 - *"djedfty shepsy chet ankh perti"* - The sacred serpent which bit Ra which caused Ra's fire of life to blow out"

Verse 29 - *"im f djezef der nez Imy na ashu"* - "Into himself as he was overpowered by it even now as he is in his domain as cedar"

So she set up this Taffy Shepsy she created, she kneaded it into one pointedness, she placed it on the road but it was not moving so Ra didn't even notice that it was there. So in Verse 27 he was going through the sky as he usually does, we know he was going to be at a given point and she put it there and the sacred serpent fooled him and bit him, attacked him. So think about what happened, the serpent prepared by Aset was not moving and was so quiet it became part of the background as it was not engaging with the rest of the world; in other words, it blended in. So too this practice blends in with the world as an aspirant practices this stillness and nobody in the world needs to know about it even when they are going about their duties in the world and the author of the world will not suspect that there is some part of the world that is somewhere stealthily lying in wait to make a move for spiritual liberation, a sort of spiritual break out from the jail of illusory time and space. In this context, consider that if there is firm "seatedness" (establishment in the throne of Aset) in the stillness of Spirit within, there is stillness no matter what may be happening in the illusory external world of time and space. This is the goal to be striven for.

Figure 23: Solar Boat of King Khufu built of cedar -view 1- referring to the solar boat of Ra

Figure 24: Solar Boat of King Khufu view 2

Now the "chet ankh perti" the "chet ankh" started to come forth. The "perti" is like the term "Pert M Heru" come forth by day. So he started bleeding internally. Ra's internal nature is the entire Creation as we are going to find out later. So he is bleeding into the world, bleeding into himself. This makes it possible to even get more power. So you hurt Ra and realize that we're getting to the allusion, doing some foreshadowing into the future. Ra says he has created the Gods and Goddesses, he has created people and he is actually, as we will learn in the separate scripture of the Creation that creation actually occurs by him turning himself into creation. So creation is God and God is everything that we see; let me put that idea out there and we'll start building on it. I discussed this the last time, the term Pantheistic (God as a god in Creation). We talked about how Ra exists in creation; we didn't get to the Panentheistic aspect yet. We're so far dealing with Panentheism (God as a god in Creation and transcending Creation. Since that is the case, my point is that when you get to a point when you can start nibbling at Ra, drawing some of his life force that is like a positive reinforcement feedback. You are going to get more power, more to use to go after him, to hurt him. We are using the terms hurt and attack and go after him and this is in a good way because we are hurting an illusion. That's basically what it is. We are attacking an illusion. We are trying to bring him down. He is in his boat of cedar, cedar is a red wood so that's why we call it, using that term.

Figure 25: The Third Phase of Ra: Ra-Tem

So Ra is coursing through the sky. Now he is in the form of Ra-Tem and he is getting old and he's drooling all over the place. He move's on and Lady Aset comes and collects the drool (leaking life-force of Ra) and she starts building that Taffy Shepsy. She places it on the path of Ra. Ra comes through again "Oh" he didn't watch where he was going so he falls down sick and this is the throne of cedar; also, this is another allusion to the sun in the evening which is always more red because of the position of the earth and the atmosphere. So the color is more white in the morning, more kind of yellowish bright in the mid-day and in the evening that's when he is really vulnerable. That's when you (divine serpent you created) make your move. But the move is daily, it's not like just one time you are going to attack Ra (illusoriness of Creation). This refers to the spiritual disciplines and meditation practices that should be considered as a daily process and not a one-time or event oriented ideal just as Ra's movement is daily so too the practice is daily.

Figure 26: (on following page) Artistic modern concept illustration of Ra getting Bitten by Aset's Serpent

SECTION 8: SHEDY OF WISDOM (SEBAIT - PHILOSOPHY) DISCIPLINE OF UNDERSTANDING THERE IS A SECRET NATURE OF GOD (RA) THAT WAS HITHERTO UNKNOWN AND NEEDS TO BE DISCOVERED IN ORDER TO ATTAIN THE GOAL OF LIFE.

Verse 47 - *"sa ur maut n atef ren"* - "as I am the son of a Great one" We are skipping ahead now in the scripture. Ra, at this point, is sick. He is basically telling his Gods and Goddesses, his children what happened. Basically he starts to allude to here now, and there is no reason for him to be discussing this except for us the reader to know, about who he is and presumably, how could such an illness happen to someone with his stature and origin. The Gods and Goddesses didn't know about the cause of his illness or about the nature of his being either. I guess as we heard also they don't know about his nature. So now we are being told "sa ur maut n atef ren" I am the son of a great one the essence of my father is my name." This term maut this is the same term as maut - the essence, the moral of a story. So the story of Ra is really his essence which is the source that gave birth to him or we may also say, gave rise to him. Now we are learning the truth. Now we are coming to figure out that Ra is not who we thought he was. Actually he is the child of somebody; he is an emanation of something, now he's admitting to it. He's not admitting it to Aset yet, and he is not saying who that is yet, that he emanated from, but he is telling his Gods and Goddesses, whom he gathered around to try and help him with the illness. In a way, he is saying things as a person who is feverish and that has caused him to spill some beans about his deeper nature; So by doing this practice it forces Creation (Ra) to give up secrets about its nature and thus lead to mental illumination about the mysteries of Creation. So he was delusional, in a sense, because he was sick and having delusions causing him to say things he would not ordinarily say. "How can this happen to me? I'm the son of a Great One and I'm Great too!" etc., etc., etc.

Verse 48 - *"anuk ashau renu ashatu kheperu"* - "I have many names and countless forms that are also my creation; and those are"

Verse 49 - *"Khepera - a unu m neter neb nas"* "Those are my reflections that manifest in the form of all the Gods and Goddesses". So now we are being told first of all in Verse 47 that Ra has a different parentage, he is not the Supreme One, so this is a different concept from the basic mythic wisdom about a High God who is Creator and supreme; this is where the Paraclete comes in. This is like a face man, a stand up for the real power, like the well, I wanted to get into a kind of analogy but this is like a face man like a person who is like a public relations representative. The company puts out a company relations (public relations, i.e. propaganda) person out front to be the face of the company. The other teaching being given here is that he has a myriad of names, myriad of forms the "kheperus" and these are the Khepera (creation) and the reason why we can say this is the meaning is because of this determinative which is the glyph of the image. It is the same one you might see in the word the Tutankhamun has it also. It means that his creations are reflections of him.

Verse 50 - *"Temu Heru Hekenu ta iu djed atef - a"* - So he is calling out this information to his Temu aspect and to Heru Hekenu. Hekenu is an aspect of Heru (Horus, he redeemer and tutelary of enlightened royal personalities) who proclaims truths, who sings them out. So he says, "I proclaim this to Temu who is the ender of things and to Heru Hekenu who is the singer of Divine glories. That was spoken by my father." Now Ra is talking about his own father.

Verse 51 - *"Mut - a ren -a amun set m khat - a er"* - So "my father/mother gave me my name and it was hidden in my constitution, my very being itself and this was done by."

Verse 52 - *"mes -a n mery tem erdit kheperu perty"* - "It was done by one who gave birth to me and in accord with their desires it should not be permitted that the name should be divulged. Lest be created, might be allowed that someone gain power, seize and gain power over me." So Ra is talking about his father/mother parent, so it's a kind of androgynous parent that gave him his name, and they hid it in his body, in his very being. In Neterian (Ancient Egyptian Mystery Religion) philosophy, the "name" of a thing is knowledge of the essential nature beyond outward or physical appearances – it is the deeper truth/reality of the named. They hid it particularly because they did not want anybody to find it and gain power over him or gain his same power of Creator; that is what he is letting us know. But now we are also to understand that he (Ra) is a prince and he is not "the supreme king" and that he has some Divine parent who is a mother/father over even him, meaning that they are androgynous and that they are beyond gender and they have no name and are transcendental. Realize that names relate to the realm where things can be named (time and space). What is transcending time and space cannot be named because it is beyond mind as well as time and space so names cannot occur and would not be useful anyway, again, because there is no mind to understand and cognize about them. Therefore, that transcendental divine cannot be known with the mind but it can be known as Aset is showing us the way...

Verse 54 - *"Hekau -a n Hekay er - a"* So Ra doesn't want anyone in control of his words of power that controls all creation. If that person was to gain that power by his name that is hidden by this genderless parent they could become personalities who can use those words effectively and thereby also be able to use them against him too. A person who gains these words will become like him essentially, i.e. a Creator God.

SECTION 10: SHEDY OF WISDOM UNDERSTANDING RA AND THE COSMIC FORCES ARE POWERLESS BEFORE THE MIGHT OF A SERIOUS, KHAK AB, ANTET BEGAG (DISPASSIONATE, RELENTLESS) & AN CHEN (REGULAR NOT INTERMITTENT) SPIRITUAL ASPIRANT.

You do your daily disciplines daily and you don't say, "Oh I'm just going to skip over the weekend and on Monday I'll make up for it by doing double for Saturday and Sunday." That's not "an chen".

Verse 61 - *"iu er -f mesu neter neb im khery"* - "Coming to see about Ra, his children all the gods and goddesses, his servants arrived. This term, servants, is an allusion to one of the terms referring to Priests and Priestesses. One of the names is "servant" or "hem" is another term that is used so they are his servants.

Verse 62 - *"akebu n -f iu n Aset khery khut - set"* - That's the final part of the statement, the Gods and Goddesses came in crying. He let out such a yell that it went through the heavens all through the creation, the universe and they all came from all corners of Creation to see what was going on. They were crying. They didn't know what was going on; like how when somebody is sick in the family and it is a surprise and they were in an accident and you're crying or upset and don't know how or why it happened or what will be the outcome. Some family members may not cry as they have experienced and learned much through life. It's not that you cannot cry, or show emotion, but that internally you are steady due to your feelings and thoughts being righteous instead of based on fear, sentimentalities and worldly irrational desires about life. So the Gods and Goddesses are crying but now walking in comes somebody else. "iu n Aset khery khut - set" -"Then arrived Aset who is also his servant who was not crying but instead she was provisioned with power."

Verse 63 - *"Aset ra set m nafu n ankh tjez set"* - "Residing in her mouth, in the form of breath of life her invocatory creative words of power."

tjez
creative
words

Verse 64 - *"her der mentu medtu - set s -ankh gau hetytu"* - So she comes in now provisioned with of words of power that control breath of life. We talked about before that Ra is the Creator of breath of life and fire of life, conscious awareness. The breath of life is what allows your body to be alive, to be conscious, and the fire of life is what allows it to do work. That's the kind of difference that you can think about. So you can be alive but you may not be able to move around and do work or do anything. You may not be able to build anything. This is why Aset "has the power to revive Asar later in the Asarian Resurrection myth. She is using "tjez"; this word I want you to remember is a

creative kind of dynamic symbol of the words but this ⟨knot glyph⟩ "tjez" symbol, especially this knot symbol; this is a knot and it means to be able to tie things together. So if you are able to tie life force together into something, you can bring it alive. You can tie two atoms together, you can create molecules. You can also tie up life force energy with your aryu to create a life on earth along with situations, relations, and events in life. This is the creative process. She has some of that creative power from Ra and from her spiritual practices of khak-ab dispassion and detachment which allow her to not squander her life force in worldly endeavors and relationships. It is also giving us some of the quality of this power that she has. It can remove mucous the kind of mucous that gets stuck in your throat, that makes it hard for your to breathe, that is stifling you, that is choking you, killing you, as in inflammation that leads to diseases like cancer, alzheimers, etc.. So she has the power to remove swelling in the body and of course swelling of the mind as well.

SECTION 12: SHEDY OF ACTION, AND WISDOM AND MEDITATION (LASER FOCUS ON GOAL OF LIFE) ASET UNDETERRED, ASKS RA FOR HIS NAME AS A CONDITION FOR PROVIDING THE CURE.

So she is "divinely extorting" him and for a good cause you can beat him up, you can stick him, you can bleed him out, etc.

Verse 78 - *"Djed in Aset n Ra Aa! Djed n - a ren a k"* - "Words spoken by Aset to Ra." "Hey, tell to me the name yours." These are the special words of power of this scripture. "Djed n - a ren a k; Djed n -a ren a k this is what you would be relentlessly asking Ra, tell me your name, tell me your name! It then continues in Verse 79

Verse 79 - *"Atef Neter Neter ankh z-a demu tu her"* - "tell me your name, divine father, the divine name." So she is making sure to specify. I ask you your name and you tell me Ra, I don't want to hear that. I want to hear the divine name. She explains this teaching to Ra but it is for us, by saying: "There is life for one who affirms their personality's name." Thus we are to affirm our spiritual name and not affirm the time and space name we were given at birth. Doing this leads to divine realization while the other reinforces the time and space delusions about who we are, which is not really living (from a higher perspective).

Verse 80 - *"ren -f ankh ari pet ta"* - This is next section for when Ra starts replying. So she said "there is life for one who affirms their name." Therefore, for a person who affirms the spiritual name, there is life, meaning immortality, true life and for those who don't there is death. There is the end of this existence and that is it. Reincarnation is the other path. So then Ra starts replying, he starts trying to blow her off and starts trying to dissuade her and to evade the question.

Verse 81 - *"Nuk ari pet ta"* He starts with the same nonsense as before. "I am the Creator of the Heavens and the Earth. Here's that term again, "tjez" remember I told you before, this creative power, the knot of being able to tie things together. Keep that in mind.

It means - Interweaver. *"tjezu duu qemamu un - en tenu her f"* "I am the interweaver and constructor of the mountains and all physical creation. One who puts together interconnects and creates things and brings them into existence." That's who I am, that's what you're asking right?

SECTION 13: SHEDY OF ACTION, MEDITATION, WISDOM RELENTLESS INSISTENCE (ANTET BEGAG) AND NOT BEING DISSUADED (that is key) AFTER BEING ASKED ABOUT HIS NAME, RA TRIES IN A FUTILE EFFORT TO DISSUADE ASET BY OFFERING MORE MISINFORMATION, SUPERFICIAL APPEARANCE AND ILLUSION INSTEAD OF REALITY AND TRUTH ABOUT HIS NATURE AND NAME. THIS SECTION CULMINATES WITH RA PROCLAIMING HIS THREE MAIN FORMS (VERSES 82-94).

So he is treating Aset like a child basically. A child (2-3 yr.) comes up and asks you, "Why is the moon up in the sky?" Are you going to say, because of gravity, and because of how the moon is composed, and it's falling towards the earth but forward motion keeps it in its place? Go through all that with a 2 or 3 yr. old? You say there's a man in the moon with cheese and he's pushing the moon along. The kids say ok, that sounds good. So he is treating her like a child and trying to dismiss her. And this is how the world treats ignorant human beings who go on asking questions without will to follow through and force themselves to seek out the answers. He starts saying, I am the maker of water, and other issues in all these verses 82-94. I am the Creator of the Great Flood of the Nile; I make sexual pleasures possible, would you like to have sex, I made that.

Go for it, go and have sex and enjoy yourself; don't think about these deep issues of philosophy like my name and all that. I place the souls of the gods and goddesses inside the Creation. When I open my eyes light exists, when I close them it becomes dark. I am the source, the cause that Hapy (Nile river) flows. Not even the Gods and Goddesses know my true name. I create time. I created space.

Verse 92 - *"Nuk Khepera m dauu Ra m ahau - f" "I am Khepera the Creator in the morning, I am Ra the Sustainer at noontime and I am Temu the Completer in the evening."* These three forms relate to Ra's aspects as Creator, sustainer, and dissolver. In a cosmic sense he also brings Creation itself at zep tepy, the first time, in the beginning, and now over billions of years Creation it is sustained by Ra-Herakhty and in the end Ra in the form of Ra-Tem will bring this particular Creation to a close by dissolving it back into the primeval ocean, the Nun, what modern physicists may refer to as dark matter and dark energy.

Verse 94 - *"an khesef metut m shemi set an nedjem neter aah"* - *"After all these things that were said there was no effect on the poison that was killing Ra and it did not go marching away out of his body like a defeated army. So Ra the great god was not relieved of his pain at all."* This term "nedjem" means something sweet, something positive, some good feeling, pleasure from a physical standpoint. So after all this was said, he was not helped, and he was not benefitted by all his continued lies. He's trying to give her more illusions, in other words. He's trying to give her more illusions to try and dissuade her instead of giving her the truth which is what she is seeking. So Aset is undeterred.

Verse 95 - *"Djed in Aset n Ra an Ren k ipu"* - Now this is Speech of Aset after he told her all this nonsense. *"This Isis said to Ra in all those things you told me, the whole catalog of things you itemized, I did not hear your name."*

Verse 96 - *"m na died k n-a A djed k set n-a"* - *"I don't hear your name in those things you told me. Oh Ra I ask thee again to tell me your Divine name."*

Verse 97 - *"Pery ta metut ankh z-a"* - *"The poison is removed and life is restored to a person when they"*

Verse 98 - *"demu tu ren-f "*- *"affirm it. When they unequivocally state their Divine name."* Come on Ra, come on. Let's finish this.

SECTION 15: RA RELENTS AND AGREES TO OPEN HIMSELF UP FOR ASET TO ENTER HIM AND DISCOVER HIS REAL NAME. HERE ENDS THE LOWER MEDITATION PRACTICE AND THE GOAL OF THE SACRED SERPENT HAS BEEN ACHIEVED DISARMING RA (CREATION) AND ALLOWING ITS ESSENTIAL NATURE TO BE DISCOVERED BY JOINING WITH IT. SO AT THIS POINT THERE ARE NO MORE THOUGHTS, CHANTS OR CONCENTRATIONS OR FOCUS ON THE IMAGES OF RA, RATHER THE DISCIPLINE NOW IS CONTEMPLATION OF THE ABSTRACT AND UNDIFFERENTIATED ESSENCE OF EXISTENCE EVERYWHERE AND IN ALL THINGS AND AS ONESELF.

Verse 102 - *"Djed in Hem n Ra dit n-a"* - *"His Majesty, Ra, said, I freely give myself over."*

Verse 103 - *"hehuty a ma Aset pert ren a m"* - *"to be looked through without obstruction or obfuscation."* So now there are no more tricks, there are no more delusions, no more evading. *"My name shall come forth which is in"*

Verse 104 - *"khat a - er khat -z Amun n su netery m"* - *"my body and it shall pass to the body of Isis, for it cannot be spoken with words since there are no words that can describe it or contain it. Having said that, the divine being Ra became hidden within."* We will find out what that hiddenness means later. Now Ra is saying, "Ok I'm going to allow myself to be searched so Aset can come into me now and search. At this point the purpose of the one pointedness has broken through and it has not just delivered poison. Now it has caused Ra and Creation itself to start tumbling down.

Now we are moving into an area that is beyond thoughts, beyond feelings, beyond chants, beyond jokes, beyond lies, this is a region called "An rut f" where there are no more thoughts, no more concepts, no more ideas, now there is nothing but conscious awareness beyond forms. But that truth is beyond words so you have to experience it, you have to be it and you have to discover it. This is likened to very quickly, the region of the human psyche that is known as deep, dreamless sleep. In deep, dreamless sleep you do not have forms. You are not dreaming and you are not awake, you are just kind of there, kind of floating in an undifferentiated ocean but you are not conscious of it. That's the difference. That's like the Nun region itself. If you are conscious of it then we call it, "An rut f". You are not aware of yourself as an individual, you are aware as an entity that exists as consciousness awareness itself. Within that mass, there is an un-named being, what is called "Neter an Ren" -Divine without name, without form. Whatever that is that we cannot name it or describe it that is what is discovered, that is what or who is the source, the substratum of all Creation, the substratum of Nun, Primeval Waters, the stuff that everything is made of and that is the higher reality of Ra. Once a person reaches that meditative state they have to be in there and allow that Divine Self to be revealed. That is what is called knowing Ra. Notice that Ra is saying he is allowing himself to be searched through. But he is not giving it, she still has to go to experience the name and also notice that she has not given him any antidote yet so

Ra (Creation) is still in a state of weakness, of being compromised, making him cooperative and conciliatory instead of defiant, powerful and elusive.

Verse 105 - *"Neteru usech Aset m uia n hehu"* - So then he became hidden in his gods and goddesses which means that Ra is the essence of the gods and goddesses, the Neteru, which are cosmic forces of nature manifesting as the physical creation we see all around us. So when Ra gave himself over and said I give up, his outward manifestation just withdrew into nature itself- which also is his Creation made out of himself anyway. But the power of Ra to project the illusoriness of Creation was withdrawn. His image as this God who is sitting there on the throne and on his boat, that is the outward manifestation of a Creator divinity and that is being set aside now because we now know the truth about what (Creation) and who (transcendental divinity without a name) he really is. "His throne in the boat of millions of years was empty and he was not to be seen. Having succeeded through the last test of will, Aset went passed the illusory creations of and manifestation of Ra and now also passed the illusory identity as embodied in a divine Creator personality as a God concept of myth and ritual and concept in the mind (differentiated consciousness). Now she is entering a state of awareness at the level of undifferentiated consciousness, *An rut f,* a void of thoughts and concepts, the deeper region of which is to be found the source of all Ra's divinity.

===================== Philosophical Point =====================

Just a philosophical point, we are studying a combination of the Aset tradition and Ra Anunian tradition; if you go into the Asarian Tradition and go into *An rut f* you find Asar. So by whichever name the particular tradition calls it, the divinity is the same one you find there. That is the ultimate, the absolute, the unnamable transcendental being upon which the Creator and the Creation both rest just as when you have a dream you are the Creator and you are also the Creation. So there is no contradiction, it is the same One Divine Source. Akhenaton acknowledged that the source of the Aton is the same source of all the Gods and Goddesses, and all the other gods and goddesses from other countries as well. So the process of spiritual evolution as outlined in the Scripture of Aset and Ra is of going beyond this level of identity of this embodied, divine personality, a god, a paraclete, a head of a henotheistic system of gods and goddesses and entering a void of undifferentiated consciousness, *An rut f,* where is to be found the source of all Ra's divinity and thus becoming one with the essence of that which is described as the Father/Mother Divine (this divine essence is also described earlier as "Neter" (Divinity, or Divine Self). Neter may also be described as "the undifferentiated, transcendental Divine that is hidden within time and space".

===================

Mysteries of Isis and Ra

SECTION 16: HAVING ACHIEVED THE GOAL TEMU'S THRONE IS VACANT (that's the image below, the top image is original and I removed Temu (from the center of the sundisk) to give you the impression of what the scripture means) **AND HE IS NO LONGER THE SOLE RULER OF CREATION. ASET MADE A PACT with Ra.**

Summary: The work of the Taffy Shepsy is done, the goal, the fruit of all that work and labor that she did, the dispassion and detachment and relentless pursuit of the mystery behind Ra, all that was effective. So now Aset is in control and she makes the rules. So she is dictating a pact WITH RA TO USE HER INTUITIONAL WISDOM TO PROVIDE THE TEACHING OF ENLIGHTENMENT TO HERU WHEN ITS TIME TO COME FORTH (ENLIGHTENMENT).

Figure 27: Tem in his boat and then absent

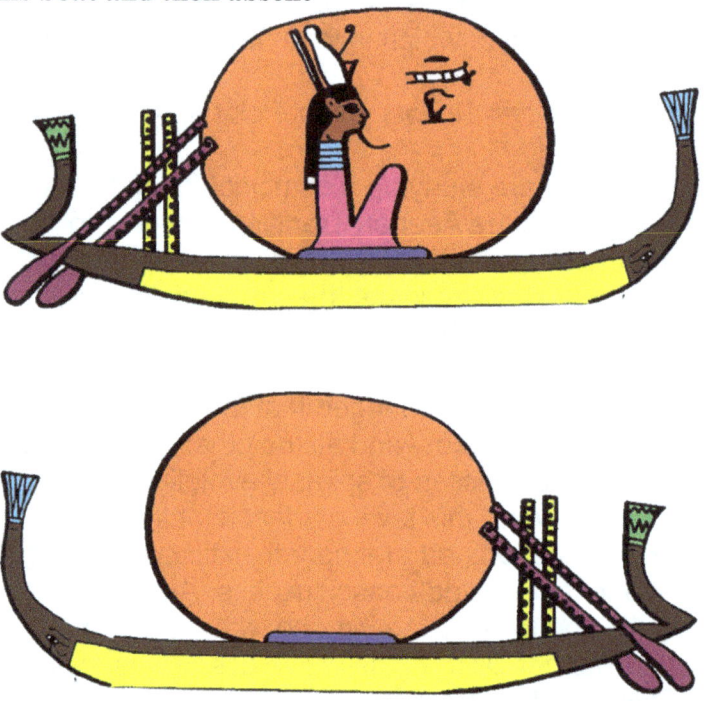

Verse 106 - *"ar kheperu mi zep pert net"* - *"As regards to a time that will come in the future"* [This is alluding to the Asarian Resurrection when there is going to be a battle between Set and Heru who is going to be born and he's also at one point going to get killed and die and be revived.] *"A time that is created like the time of the first creation when there will be a coming forth of"*

Verse 107 - *"ab djed z n sa Heru zenhau net su"* Coming forth of the heart as described in the Pert M Heru the Book of Coming Forth and becoming Heru. *"for that time due to what has been done here, now let there be a compact of the"*

Verse 108 - *"m ankh neter erdat neter maa fy"* - *"a compact of he in a life oath with the divinity when the time comes the divinity will give his two eyes."* So when the time comes Ra is going to give his two eyes which means his cosmic mind and Life Force, his life force to Heru when he will need them. That's what we are really alluding to. Now that Aset has achieved this great goal, now she is saying I want also a pact, an agreement between myself and Ra that in a future time when my son Heru is going to come to a point in his life where he is going to be like me. Where he is going to want to become enlightened and he's going to want to overcome the battle of life. This is what this term "zep" means, "time" and this term "ar Kherperu mi zep" this relates to a term called "zep tepy", "tepy" means the first or the one from the beginning so "zep tepy" means time from the beginning; i.e. In the time of the beginning. Remember in the story of Hetheru and Djehuty where it said at the end to meditate in a circle and the symbol of Ra and visualize yourself as Ra as he was in the beginning. This teaching is in a way related and compatible with other teachings; so as to the question of which mythic wisdom teaching one should pursue, it's a question of which one suits your personality best. Choose the teaching that most interests and excites the spiritual devotion and intellect.

Another point is, when you come to that time when you are enlightened nothing matters, that happened in your life before, you are becoming like you were in the time of your own beginning, before becoming an ego personality, separate and forgetting your primeval divine nature; that is your enlightenment, the time of your beginning because you have transcended time and space, you are in eternity, and there is no beginning or end in eternity, that is only for bodies in time and space. So she is saying when the time comes I want this same possibility for Heru.

SECTION 18: SHEDY OF NEHAST [Enlightenment] NEFER HETEP RESTING IN THE DIVINE ABODE THRONE OF RA ASET RESTORES RA TO HEALTH WITH SPECIAL WORDS OF POWER TO HEAL THE MIND AND SOUL HURT BY THE DELUSIONS OF LIFE AND THEREBY ALLOWS CREATION TO REVERT BACK TO ITS ILLUSORY FORM AND RA RETURNS TO CREATING, SUSTAINING AND CONCLUDING THE DAYS AND YEARS AS BEFORE.

About what I said before, that when you attain enlightenment it doesn't matter what you did before in your previous life; It doesn't matter what ignorance you lived by before, as long as you follow the path that leads to enlightenment, all that is seen as illusory. It doesn't mean that a person can be unrighteous or follow delusions like faith-based religion or atheism or criminality, sentimentality, etc. and still attain enlightenment as if those things don't matter. You still need to be righteous to attain enlightenment. That's something different. You still have had to work to cleanse yourself, you have moved beyond illusions and delusions of life so therefore you recognize the illusion of things of the past both bad and good.

Verse 114 - *"Ra ankh-f metut mer"* - *"Ra may live he, and the poison dies." "May Ra live and the poison die".* Having achieved the goal of life, the fruit of her dispassion, detachment and concentration on this form, function and nature, the one pointed sacred serpent discipline had served its purpose; Now the world was no longer a source of delusion since her existence is now like that of Ra. The magician is not deluded by his/her own magic. Those who learn the secret of the magician are in on it with them and they partake in the knowledge of the magic. The Creation is the illusion weaved by the magician and if the trick is understood the magician is not deluded by his/her own magic and in reality there was no spell, just ignorance of the fact that there is an illusion going on and ignorance about the secret of that illusion. So Ra and the Creation can continue without deluding her." Therefore, she can allow the world to continue. She had stopped the world when she entered the *An rut f* of Ra (so all perceptions of the world as a reality ceased during that period); now she has dual consciousness, about her previous life and now also about the nature of her/The Higher Self, so it is ok for the world to go on, meaning that she can come back to the world of time and space reality and interact with people, and not be troubled by the world or deluded by worldly relative realities.

Verse 115 - *"tjist"* - *"and reciprocally bound firm. There's a child of a certain woman"*

Verse 116 - *"ankh -f metut mer djed n Aset ur"* - *"that for that child of that woman when the time comes may the poison die in him too. These words are spoken by Isis, the Great."* So you remember that Heru was poisoned in the Asarian Resurrection, so when that time comes may she get help to deal with that. But for now, Ra can go back and continue being Ra, as we have known him, as a Creator, sustainer, and dissolver of Creation.

SECTION 19: ASET PROVIDES INSTRUCTIONS FOR ANYONE WISHING TO FOLLOW THIS PATH BY A RITUAL THAT INCLUDES UTTERING THE WORDS OF POWER SHE USED WITH THE INTENT, FEELING, RELENTLESS INTENSITY SHE APPLIED ALL TO BE DONE IN FRONT OF SPECIAL IMAGES.

Verse 117 - *"Henut neteru rech Ra m ren f djezef"* - Now she is referred to as Mistress of Gods and Goddesses. She is not just Aset.
"The mistress of the Gods and Goddesses she who is the knower of Ra's own Divine name!" (This is her new title added to her other ones)

Verse 118 - *"Djed medu her tu n Temu hena Heru Hekenu"* - "She instructs that these words of the teaching are to be spoken over an image of the god Temu along with an image of Heru the Proclaimer and"

<u>Final verse:</u>
Verse 119 - *"repyt Aset tut Heru"* - "also over an image of the glorious and extolled goddess Isis together with an image of Heru."

SUMMARY:
That is what we have here. This is a poster that I've created here based on the scripture. All of these glyphs that you see here are based on the scripture of Aset and Ra, the temple scripture that we've been using. This here is "djed n -a ren -a k" "Tell to I the name" Then "atef neter neter" "father divine, the divine name". This is the Taffy Shepsy down here in the center. I'm going to cover this in more detail so this is a quick overview and have every single thing mapped out for you. This means "mit" means death. The ankh means life. This is the Taffy Shepsy movement. Ra and Aset. Once you go through the process of building and successfully deploying the Taffy Shepsy which means that you make it, you let it sit motionlessly, and then it strikes when the time is right. It does it's work, you gain the knowledge, then you can say, "Ra ankh -f metut mer" which means that Ra may live and may the poison die. Ok so we'll go into some of the other details. You should recognize some of the other things already. That is a synopsis of the teaching of the Myth of Aset and Ra.

Figure 28: TEACHINGS OF TEMPLE OF ASET (ISIS) MEDITATION MAT/POSTER

Mysteries of Isis and Ra

Translation of the Aset Meditation Mat

1. Khepera: Morning sun
2. Ra ankh metut mer —may Ra live and may poison die
3. Ankh z-a demu –life to one who declares it
4. her ren-personality's name
5. ouaah —meditation
6. Ankh —life
7. Temu —Form of Ra in the evening
8. Anuk ari pet ta = I am creator of heaven and earth
9. Tjez nuk ari mu –I am maker of waters
10. Khepertu meht ur—creator of the great flood
11. Djed in Aset khnem Ra nedjyt sen su Asar–words by Isis I am united with Ra and protector of her brother Osiris
12. Djed in Ra Hrakhty –words spoken by Ra of the two horizons
13. Nuk ari —I am maker
14. unnu kheperu heru=of time-hours and days
15. Aset zet = Isis as woman
16. Pa remteju = the men and women
17. Khak ab=disgusted
18. Heru Sa Aset Sa Asar=Horus the son of Isis and Osiris
19. Djed na Ren a K-Tell to I name thine
20. Atef Neter Neter=Father Divine spiritual
21. Taffy Shepsy=Divine Serpent
22. Mity Mit- Likeness dies
23. Heru Hekenu
24. Menu im k=suffering illness in thee
25. Temu —the god in his sundisk-boat and then absent
26. Rechat=Lady of Wisdom
27. Mer =Death

(C)2015 Sema Institute/ Kemet University

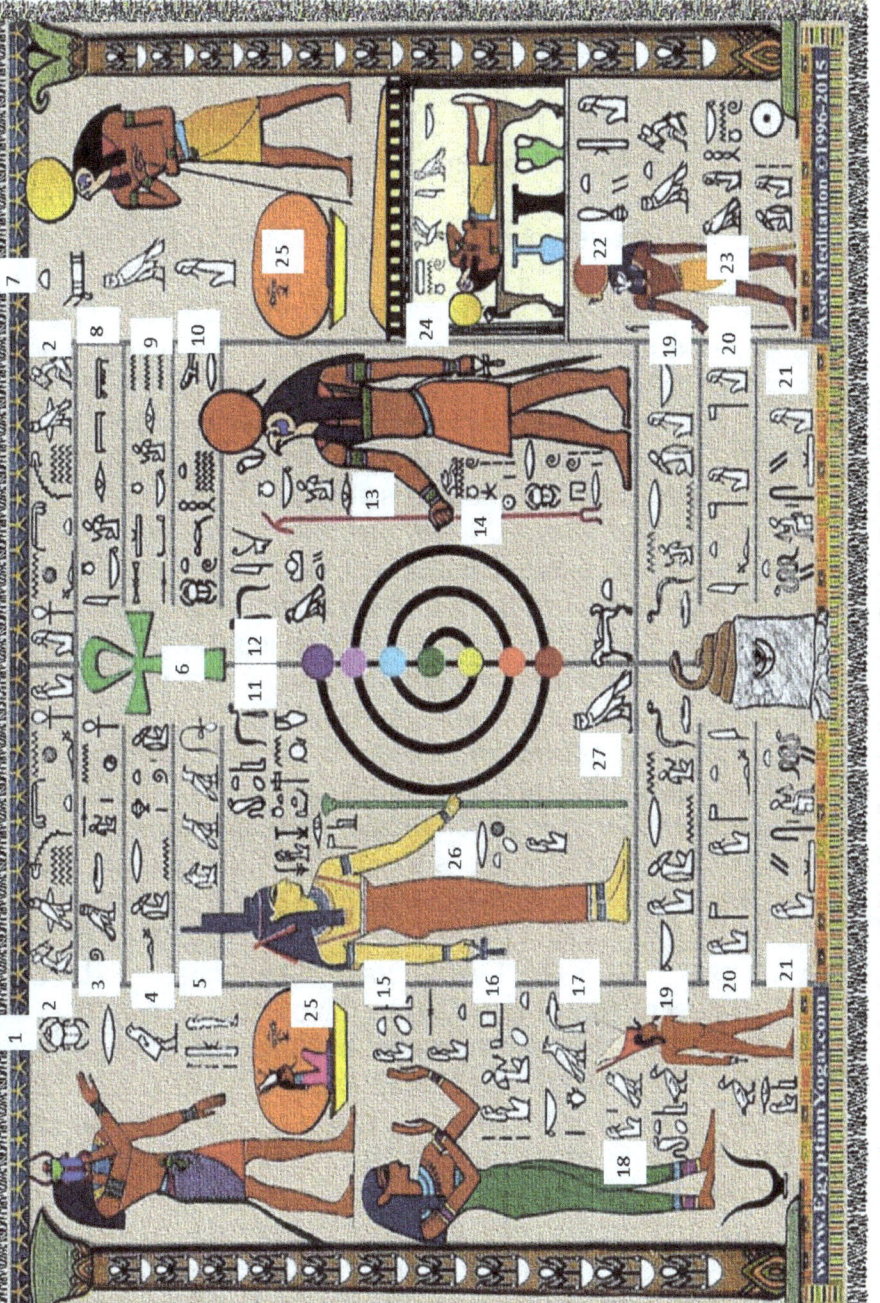

QUESTIONS AND ANSWERS

Question - Yes, so a line is coming to mind, at least part of a line from Evening Worship when it is referencing An rut f a region of the Netherworld so the question is, if it is "a region" as it is stated in the evening worship, so there must be more than one region in the Netherworld?

Sebai Maa - You talking about An rut f?

Questioner - Yes

Sebai Maa - The An rut f is only one region.

Question - No it's referencing as An rut f as being a region of the Netherworld.

Sebai Maa - Right a region. There is only one Netherworld and only one An rut f section of the Netherworld. The same region is in the netherworld and any advancing sentient being can find it in the nether regions of their own mind.

Question - Ok, so the question I'm trying to get at is, if An rut f is a state where there is no thought, then what can there possibly be beyond that?

Sebai Maa - That is a question that you don't ask with your mind. You are asking with a mind that is caught still in the terms of concepts. All you can do at this point is believe the Sages when they give descriptions and instructions on how to realize that for yourself. You are experiencing not through your mind and senses, you are experiencing as Spirit directly without mind and senses. Thus you are experiencing yourself in the primeval form, like zep tepy, before mind came into being as an opaque aspect of the personality. That is the best way to describe it butHyou have to experience it for yourself since the description is intellectual and the experience is still something else that is beyond words. What happens is that in that state or level of experience you are not thinking and when you come back here then you can say, "Oh this is like this, it felt like floating, it felt like flying, it felt like falling forever." Other poetic or metaphorical descriptions can be given. Metaphors and analogies can be used but that is as close as "it" can be described just like if a new flavor of ice-cream is put forth there are many analogies to other ice-cream experiences that can be given but the taste surpasses all descriptions. Mind you, this is just an analogy to bring a point across. Enlightenment is not like any other experience so the analogy itself is limited. But while you are there, there's no time and space and there's no cognizing ability, you cannot intellectualize and compare this to something else because there's no duality and no separate ego personality, that you can call you, since personality arises because there is duality. However, you can be conscious even without mind. So you have to come back to normal time and space awareness, back to mind usage and then you can make sense of it with your intellect through analogies and metaphors so as to describe it to others.

Question - so this is in meditation?

Sebai Maa – Yes this is the third stage of the practice given by Aset known as Listening, Reflection and Meditation. When you are immersed in your primeval nature beyond time and space and mind you are in the state of meditation.

Question - He asked how can you understand if there's no mind, no thoughts in that region how can you come back to talk about it if there's no cognition? I wanted to know that if since there is no thought my question was then what can be beyond that? Well, you're not sensing or utilizing cognition at that point, it's all Spirit. So it's gnosis.

Sebai Maa – An analogy is given to explain that. If you are in a state of deep dreamless sleep you are floating in a state of anrutef but unconsciously. However, when you wake up you remember a feeling of nothingness, not objects but also fullness but unexplainable fullness that you done experience when awake. Again, you can be conscious even without mind. So you have to come back to normal time and space awareness, back to mind usage and then you can make sense of it with your intellect through analogies and metaphors so as to describe it to others.

Let's go further into the philosophy so as to understand how far that state is from the mind and its concepts and ideas. Even calling it "Spirit" that's an idea. Even if we say "All Encompassing Divinity" that's a concept. Even if we say we are using a "concept," that's a concept. We have to learn how to be orderly with our philosophy and understand that there's a region where it breaks down, like when the laws of physics break down in black holes. It's like in physics there's a region where physics breaks down and they call it "black holes" but still a universe of existence operates in a black hole because there is a singularity there but it transcends all the laws of physics and mental descriptions and yet physicists claim it exists. They cannot explain it but they can understand intellectually about it. So this transcends all the laws of language to describe or cognize. You can listen to all the descriptions and once you go and experience it for yourself then you can make sense of it afterward but not in words but in intuitional knowing. Then you say, "Oh wow that was All Encompassing". "Oh it was everything, it was non-dual." All these are good approximate concepts but they still don't have anything to do with the actual reality which you have to go in and experience like Ra told Aset to do. Anything you think of in your mind, any concept is in the realm of time and space which is limited and therefore illusory. They can be useful but in the ultimate experience they are to be transcended.

Question - So does this un-describable come to one through meditation?

Sebai Maa - Yes that is what we're talking about. But this is a process. Don't think of meditation as only I'm going to sit down here and close my eyes and chant. That is part of it. You have to cleanse your unconscious mind, you have to direct yourself and become dispassionate about the world. It's a whole process that you are building. That is called building the Taffy Shepsy. All of this is a meditative process, as I said before, the listening to the teaching that's part of the meditation system, reflecting on it and after you leave here, thinking about it again and again. You should promote thinking like, "Wow what he said in the lecture that was really something." That's the reflective process and every time you do that, if you truly understand, you are neutralizing ignorance and cleansing ignorance and you're putting positive Aryu in the mind and that is going to eventually lead to a reduction of negative energy and negative desires that cloud the mind and promote agitation and inability to concentrate. The Aryu are like clouds that are blocking you from realizing the higher truth of your sky-like existence. So this is a process. Meditation is the process but it's a kind of holistic process, not just like sitting and meditating and not reflecting and not learning the philosophy and not applying it; all of it must be practiced together for success. Ultimately, you are to progress to be able to have this high experience spontaneously without having to think about it or meditate and even when your senses and mind are engaged in activities in time and space-this is the final stage reached by Aset.

Also, there's the point which was mentioned the fact that when you are intensively practicing, the practice doesn't stop at some exactly marked point. Like, say you were meditating but now you have to go to work, if you are intense with your spiritual practices, the effect of those practices is still working even when you are doing other things. For example, if you are a doctor, it doesn't stop when you are not doing doctor work. It is still there. So if you become versed at this level of initiatic practice it continues working regardless of whatever you are doing. You can be taking a shower and it is still working in your unconscious mind. Or you're going to work, or driving, or taking care of your child if you are that level of intensity, understanding and devotion of practice. So I want to give you all the idea especially with this teaching, this is given as a kind of teaching in a short period of time but this is a process that is powerful and can be effective if you take it day by day, and step by step and act at the higher intensity gradually. That is what it is for.

Question- And what is the effect of these spiritual practices?

Sebai Maa - I give myself over to Aset so she can search me, that's the effect.

Question- There's different levels, the path or the consciousness, the Path of Divine Love, please correlate that to this plane or level of consciousness?

Sebai Maa - The Path of Divine Love leads to the same goal but through a different pathway, through the pathway of emotions and feelings and a relationship with the Divine as a lover, as a mother, father, as a child. In this practice, there is wisdom also but feelings are more prominent while being vetted by wisdom. In the path of wisdom, there are emotions and emotions support the wisdom and intellectual practice. All those kinds of love, just mentioned, come together in one All Encompassing Love which is what Neter Merri means it means Divine Love. All of Creation is Love because, think about it, that is what every human being is directed to, desiring. Every human being is intrinsically desiring to acquire or to join with some aspect of Creation to find fulfillment and happiness, in other words, they desire (love) some aspect of Creation. Since God is everywhere and everything you are actually seeking God, loving God in various forms, but not really realizing that you are seeking God. If you have Divine Love then you have realized that what you are seeking is everywhere and that is like and intensive All Encompassing kind of practice of Divine awareness and feeling all the time. You can think of it as all the paths lead to the same one destination; as an analogy like a lake and you can have a lion coming to drink water from a lake and you can have a deer that is coming from a different section. Of course, if a lion sees a deer he's going to think certain agitating thoughts right? But if they come to the lake they both share in the same lake, if they don't see each other things will be cool right? So sort of giving this to give you an idea, if you have different religions, or different paths, and you try to mix them in an inappropriate way, in a non-sagely sponsored way, there can be conflict, there can be misunderstanding, even though if they are authentic paths and practiced correctly they lead to the same destination. That is how it should be understood.

Question - When Aset created the Taffy Shepsy and set it out she must have known that he had to give her his name or already knew his name because once the poison is set Creation is going to crumble. So I'm thinking that she must've already either knew his name or had known that he had to tell her his name?

Sebai Maa – Think about it, many of you may not be enlightened but there is something you may not be able to explain that tells you deep down that there is some higher truth missing in life and that what the scripture is saying is true even if you cannot put your finger on it or explain it intellectually and that gives you impetus to move forward and pursue the goal you intrinsically know must be there. This is not a faith-based process mind you; it is a process whereby your studies have led you to conclusions that your heart tells you must be true so you set out to pursue it, to prove it, and attain it.

So when she started out she did not know his name but she did know enough from her previous studies to conclude that life and Creation are illusory and therefore there has to be something more if we reflect that we are alive so there is something real about us but the lives we are leading are bogus since life is changeable and fleeting. Therefore, there has to be something beyond, the illusory nature of Creation and that is called "the Name". So she did know that there is something more to life and knowing the name of Ra confers knowing that which is yet to be known and upon knowing which all that is to be known will be known. So she knew that there was a name because she had studied the teaching and she knew that this process would compel him to tell her the name. But she did not know the name and that is why she had to do the process of the spiritual disciplines to transform herself essentially from a worldly to spiritual directed personality. Of course, all this is for our benefit so we can know what was and is to be done and not just by her but by the priests and priestesses.

I've discussed this before in 2007 I went over it, but a couple of things might be helpful also. In the discipline of the Temple of Aset, it was told that initiates were instructed that they should spend time with the Goddess. Which means learning the teaching, placing myself as a conduit for the Goddess' teaching to come through? Therefore, spending time with her representatives is spending time with her. So in a way if I am an authentic conduit then it would be like if you sit together with me and sitting with the Goddess; Or sitting with the scripture, sitting with her image and keeping it with you close. That is one thing. That is one of the important teachings of the Temple for an initiate. The next important teaching for the Temple is that the goal of life is to seek after the nature of the Primary Being, recognize that that is the whole idea. She does not say that she is a Goddess, as a personality, because that would be like Ra also. So she is talking about the Source. This was the teaching that was given to the initiates of the Temple. There's another little lecture series on the disciplines of the temple of Aset based on the writings of Plutarch that was done in 2007. That would be a good complement to this study.

HTP

NOTE
For a more in-depth study go to the course "Teachings of the Temple of Aset" given at www.EgyptianMysterySchool.org.

THE DEEPER MEANING OF THE MYTHS OF THE GODDESS ASET-A GLOSS ON THE MYTH OF RA AND ASET

In the Ausarian Resurrection story, Asar and his reincarnation in the form of Heru is a symbol for the resurrection which must occur in the life of every human being. In this manner, the story of the Ausarian Trinity of Asar, Aset and Heru and the Egyptian Psedjet holds hidden teachings, which when understood and properly practiced, will lead to spiritual enlightenment.

So Aset is the true heroine of the entire myth relating to Asar. It was because of Aset's love, devotion, and knowledge of how to call on the Divine (Ra) that Heru, the redeemer of righteousness upon earth, was resurrected.

So what was this special nature of this goddess which allowed her to resurrect Asar and Heru, and what is the significance of this resurrection? What relation does it have to people in modern times?

The story of Ra and Aset, though short, imparts important mystical teachings of monumental proportions. First, we are introduced to the Supreme Being in the form of Ra. Ra is the essence of all Creation, the mover in motion, the wetness of water, the heat in the sun's rays, the sustaining force in the air that allows living beings to live by breath. Ra is the very root from which all emanates and is sustained. Ra sits on his barque which emerged from the Primeval Ocean. Waves form as a result of the movement of his barque. These waves are vibrations which cause all of the differentiation of matter in the world. All matter, the world itself, is essentially the Primeval Ocean, after its constituent elements have taken forms due to the vibrations produced from the motion of the barque of Ra. If Ra ceases to move in his barque the matter of the universe will be devoid of vibration and will return to an undifferentiated form.

Aset is the female manifestation of Ra. She is his daughter. Aset lived as a woman, but she evolved by learning the knowledge of the world. This knowledge is sometimes referred to as the lower mysteries. It relates to information about the physical world, human interaction and human life. Sciences such as engineering, medicine, anthropology, history, social interactions, politics, economics, etc., are related to human beings and to the relative world. They are changeable and subject to error. The use of the word "relative" here implies the understanding that all worldly knowledge has a practical value as long as the world exists, and as long as there is human life. However, what sciences were there before the world and human beings came into existence and which sciences will be there after the world and human beings cease to exist? The answer is none. Further, what use is science to someone who is asleep or dead? The answer is none. Therefore, worldly knowledge which is related to events in time and space are only useful in a particular reality, a particular realm of existence, and not in all places and at all times. Therefore it is referred to as relative, and as practical knowledge.

Above: The Ancient Egyptian symbol of The Primeval Ocean.

Right: The Ancient Egyptian

All existence is likened to a vast ocean because the ocean is a single all-encompassing, all-pervasive, essence which accepts all rivers without becoming full and which is the source and sustenance of all life on earth.

In the same way, all matter in the universe is part of one all-encompassing essence from which all of the different forms emerge and take shape and into which they decay and dissolve through the cycle of time.

There is a teaching in reference to a Primeval Ocean in Ancient Egyptian, Christian, Hindu and other mythologies.

Aset developed an interest in discovering the higher truths and realities. This quality is termed *spiritual aspiration*. She wanted to discover the truth which is not conditional or relative, but that which is absolute and eternal. Absolute truth is the real truth because it is not affected by time or circumstance. She knew that Ra was the higher truth because he was the Creator of the relative universe. So she began to meditate on the idea of discovering the name of her father since this was the highest truth of all.

The "mystical name" is an Ancient Egyptian philosophy which relates to understanding the essence of a thing. Everything that comes into existence receives a name, and then this thing is "known." However, there is a higher essence within all objects which is unknown. This essence is what sustains the very atoms which go to make up the objects. But what sustains the atoms? They are not self-sustaining. They come into and out of existence in accordance with a certain plan. Modern physics understands this much. Matter is not "solid" and does not have permanent existence. Energy, mass and time are all relative. These teachings were already understood in Ancient Egypt thousands of years before the development of quantum physics in modern times. The existence of matter and the plan by which it manifests is the work of Ra. This is the higher reality which Aset wanted to know.

Knowing is of two types. Something can be known intellectually. You can have vast knowledge about a subject such as scriptural writings, medical science, etc. However, this knowledge is only useful in the relative world. Mystical knowledge means understanding the very essence of existence. This knowledge transforms the knower. The knower of this kind of knowledge becomes one with the higher essence itself. Therefore, Aset was seeking to transform herself into a higher form of consciousness. So she looked up to the gods and goddesses, but even more so to the spirits, because even the gods and goddesses do not know the absolute name of Ra. Anything that is in a relative form of existence cannot know that which is absolute because the absolute is the totality and a piece cannot know the whole. All of the planes of existence are relative. There are three major planes of existence. Human life occurs in the Physical Plane. The realm of the gods and goddesses is the Astral Plane and the realm of the spirits is the Causal Plane. Beyond the Causal Plane lies the Absolute which transcends all planes. This is where the true name of Ra is to be discovered. This was Aset's true goal. For more on the planes of existence see the book *The Book of the Dead* by Dr. Muata Ashby.

Ra is the relative name of the Supreme Being. It is a metaphor or descriptive symbol of the Divine for use in the relative world. The Sages of ancient times created such symbols for the purpose of aiding the mind by providing it with an objective form on which to concentrate. The Ancient Egyptian word, *bes*, means "visible image of the god or goddess." The Self or God has no particular form or name. However, images are used for spiritual practice since it is easier at first to worship the Divine as an image. It is an image, with name and form, that is used for devotional purposes and is not to be understood as a reality. In order to grow spiritually, an aspirant needs to discover the transcendental name (essence) of the Divine, beyond the images. This occurs when the mind evolves in wisdom and spiritual sensitivity. This means gradually becoming one with the Divine. This was Aset's goal. Aset knew that any person who knows their real, divine, name will attain enlightenment. This is what she means when she says, "The person who hath declared his name shall live."

So Aset decided to stop Ra and force him to give her his absolute name. She took a part of his body (spirit) and a part of the physical universe (earth) and made it into the form of a serpent. The mixing of spirit and matter is a metaphor relating to the reunification of the opposite poles which comprise Creation. When there is vibration in matter, the world exists as a duality with opposite poles (positive and negative, attraction and repulsion, etc.). This means that there are pairs of opposites in Creation, and the mind operates within this understanding. The most important form of duality which operates in every unenlightened human being is individuality. A human being who is ignorant of the Divine Name thinks, "I am an individual, separate and distinct from the rest of the world and from God." The duality of the opposites also refers to male-female, up-down, here-there, yes-no, etc. However, before Creation came into existence there were no opposites because there was no differentiation in matter. There was just a single essence, the Primeval Ocean until Ra emerged from the ocean and started to cause ripples (vibrations) in it.

The serpent is the perfect instrument to disable the relative form of Ra. The serpent is a metaphor of the goddess and her energy or power to accomplish any and all tasks, even to stop Creation. The serpent is also a metaphor of the internal Life Force within every human being. The mystical art of awakening this power and directing it towards breaking down the obstacles of spiritual evolution (ignorance, anger, hatred, desire, jealousy, frustration) is known as the Science of the Serpent Power or Serpent Power Yoga.

So Aset's serpent bit Ra which debilitated his ability to maintain Creation. His weakness at this point of the story symbolizes the breakdown of relative knowledge. Ra's journey on the barque sustains the practical (time and space) reality. However, the power of spiritual knowledge and meditation (which Aset practiced) enabled her to go beyond the relative (lower) knowledge. The bite of the serpent is a symbol of the power of wisdom and inquiry into the greatest of all questions, "Who am I?" The venomous power of this way of thinking is infallible in disarming the power of nature to delude a human being. Therefore, the study and practice of mystical philosophy, with the proper guidance, is the greatest weapon against illusion, egoism, greed, selfishness, jealousy, passion, desire, etc. These are the enemies of the soul which obstruct it in its quest to discover its unity with the Divine. It is no wonder why the serpent is the primary symbol of the Goddess in Ancient Egypt.

Thus, the relative form of Ra became weak, and his power to maintain Creation was weakened so much so that his face began to be covered over, as the land is covered during the inundation period of the Nile River. This inundation signals the dissolution of matter as it reverts to its undifferentiated state, which existed before Ra emerged from the Primeval Waters.

So Ra could not withstand Aset's probing. Nature was beginning to show its real essence. It was losing its shapes and forms. Ra allowed himself to be discovered. This discovery bestowed the knowledge of the essential nature of the Divine to Aset. This knowledge cannot be transmitted in words or even in thoughts, ideas or concepts. It is transmitted by one way alone, by communing with its source. This attainment of the special name is not a verbalization but an identification of the knower with that which is known. This is why it was transmitted from the heart of Ra to the heart of Aset and not from his mouth to her ears. This is also why it has a transformative effect on the knower.

To know the essential nature of God is to become one with God. Knowing the essential nature of God, the absolute and transcendental aspect of the Divine means becoming enlightened. Enlightenment means reaching a state of consciousness that is free from all illusion, all relativity, and all limitation. It is becoming one with God, who is omnipotent, immortal, eternal and infinite. Therefore, an enlightened Sage is internally one with the Divine even though his or her body may continue to exist in the relative world. Enlightenment or knowing the essential nature of the Divine means knowing that which when known leaves nothing else to be known. This knowledge is the source of all knowledge and the truth behind all relative truths of the world and of all human experience.

A spiritual aspirant who practices this teaching, that all existence is essentially made up of the same essence, has the power to reveal the secrets of nature and to remove the illusions of life. Also, for one who has discovered the essence of nature, it ceases to exist as such and only the higher nature remains. There is no going back to the state of ignorance once the veil of nature has been lifted. Discovering God's true nature means seeing God everywhere and in all things, including yourself as yourself beyond your ego, mind and senses. Through the process of practicing this spiritual teaching, a person's Serpent Power (Life Force Energy) is aroused. This power disables the illusoriness of the world and the negativity of one's own ego. Negativity and egoism drives people to hold on to the illusions of the world which prevents them from discovering the true essence of the Divine. The Serpent Power Energy allows a person's consciousness to go beyond the illusoriness of the world, carrying it to unite with the very source of consciousness beyond thoughts, individuality and the ego itself.

The poisoning of the relative aspect of Ra is a metaphor relating to the poisoning of an illusion. The relative form of Ra in time and space (duality) is an illusion because it is only a reflection of the Absolute. This is why Aset needed to discover the hidden, secret name. The outer name of God, that is "Ra", is not the true name but only the name for God in time and space. When God is discovered in the transcendental essence the name is un-utterable and transcendental and can only be known, experienced, in the heart. This is the absolute name of the Divine Self, which transcends all names and forms, religious and secular. Thus, the deeper meaning of the poisoning of Ra symbolizes the poisoning of the belief that the world, with its names and forms, is an abiding reality. When this poisoning occurs, through the practice of reflection on the wisdom teachings and by living life dispassionately and detached from objects and people, one is able to "kill" the world and discover the truth which sustains it. This is also known as the unveiling of the goddess.

Therefore, the uniting of one's own mind with the Cosmic Mind (The Self-God), meaning the movement away from dualistic thinking and moving closer to the understanding of the oneness which underlies all Creation allows the mind to poison or undermine (sabotage) the power of the illusion of the world. The illusion of dualistic and ignorant thinking is that God has a particular form and that everything in Creation is separate from everything else. Just as waves in the ocean are all rooted in one ocean, and just as your mental thoughts are rooted in your single mind, every object in this universe is rooted in one sustaining essence.

A spiritual aspirant must learn to see the world and the ego as illusions. Then he or she will be in a position to discover their dreamlike quality. The more a person affirms that the ego is real and that it can be satisfied by acquiring wealth and fulfillment of egoistic desires and pleasures, the more its effects appear real to the mind. However, no matter how intense a person's ego becomes, or how wealthy, famous or powerful a person becomes, death is always looming in the shadows. This in itself points to the illusoriness of the ego. That which is finite cannot be real. Therefore, the ego and the world are like the personality we become when having a dream. The world we experience when awake is like the world we experience when asleep and having a dream. They are both illusory. A spiritual aspirant must learn to develop such a powerful intellect that he / she will be able to peer through the illusoriness of the concepts and beliefs of the mind. This movement is what ultimately leads to spiritual enlightenment.

Aset was able to realize (experience) the highest truth by practicing the disciplines of Yoga. Through the power of the Yoga of Wisdom, which relates to acquiring spiritual (intuitional) knowledge and right thinking, she realized that she could attain the higher level of consciousness if she could discover the higher essence of Ra. Aset also developed the power of dispassion and detachment from the world which allowed her to turn away from human life and from the Astral Plane of the gods and goddesses as well. She was able to realize that she could discover the highest secrets of Creation if she could unite the opposites (Yoga of Tantrism). Through her devotion to truth and penetrating inquiry (Yoga of Wisdom and Meditation) into Ra's essential nature, she was able to direct all of her attention towards the Divine and pierce the *veil of illusion* (the outer form of an object).

Even though Ra gave her an answer the first time she asked for his name, Aset knew that this was only the temporal (relative) name. Her attainment in wisdom and her higher intuition allowed her to know that what he said was not the higher teaching she wanted. Ra stated that he was the Creator of the gods at the two horizons, meaning all that exists within Creation including the gods and goddesses. Therefore, even the knowledge of the gods and goddesses is lower knowledge of time and space. Ra has three forms. He is the morning sun, the creator of the day. He is the noon day sun, the sustainer of the day. He is also the evening sun or the dissolution of the day. These descriptions refer to the twenty-four hour cycle of each day, but in a broader sense, they also refer to human life and to Creation itself. Ra sustains an individual's life from birth to adulthood, and then to death. He also is the cause of the universe coming into existence from the undifferentiated Primeval Ocean which is formless, boundless and infinite, its sustenance over a period of billions of years and its ultimate dissolution back into the undifferentiated Primeval Ocean. These three states of life and Creation are relative because they are conditioned by time and circumstance. What is the nature of the entity who sustains those states but is not affected by them or changed in any way, who is the same in the beginning, middle and end? This is the question which Aset was seeking to answer.

Even though one of Ra's years are like one hundred and twenty-five human years in the realm of time and space, what is that as compared to eternity? Eternity and infinity were Aset's real goal and not relativity and the temporal nature of Creation. Aset was after that which is absolute, and not that which is perishable and fleeting. Even a billion years is an infinitesimal speck as compared to eternity. Many spiritual aspirants and the masses of people accept the exoteric teaching of a philosophy as the highest truth, but there is an esoteric philosophy behind the myth. This esoteric or inner teaching is the higher teaching meant for those who are ready to realize the higher truth. It is possible to attain a level of consciousness within which one can exist for a period equal to Ra's lifespan, but even this is ultimately perishable, fleeting and illusory.

So when people seek immortality in the realm of time and space or believe that their religion or knowledge is the "real" one or that their picture of God is the "real" one, they are engaging in nothing but ignorance. They are chasing after an illusion. The various forms of the Divine presented in all religions are nothing but symbols. Religious philosophy is only a concept to help an individual turn his/her mind towards the Divine. Symbols and religions are concepts to assist the mind, leading it to discover the higher, transcendental reality. However, those who are un-initiated into the higher teaching and accept the myth on faith will be limited in their spiritual attainment. They will be prone to egoism and erroneous thinking based on the limited powers of their minds and lower desires. They will be susceptible to the greed, animosity, anger, jealousy, and hatred of the lower self and thus, they will always be in conflict with themselves and with others. They will repudiate the myths and spiritual philosophy of others and see themselves as the followers of the truth.

An advancing spiritual aspirant, someone who has begun to unite the opposites, begins to see beyond the exoteric form of all religions. He or she begins to understand that the true object of devotion in all religions is the same Supreme Being in its absolute essence. No matter what part of the universe the religion may come from, it is the same Divinity which is being sought through the myths and symbols which are based on specific cultures and traditions. Therefore, the enlightened Sage sees no contradiction in any religion or in any form of worship as long as it is moving towards the realization of the transcendental Self. All forms of worship which fall short of this will be limited.

So Ra agrees to allow himself to be searched and discovered. Aset then assumes all of his power and glory. This is the possibility for all who seek to discover the Divine. This act of assuming the higher personality is in reality the act of becoming who you really are. It means breaking the identification you have with your relative lower self and discovering your transcendental Higher Self (Heru). This is the act of becoming an enlightened personality.

Becoming an enlightened personality does not mean that the practical world comes to an end. This is why Aset, though having come into the knowledge of Ra and having assumed equal power, cures him and allows him to continue sustaining the practical, relative reality. In the same manner, a Sage, though internally experiencing the higher reality, continues to live and exist in the practical reality, assisting others in making their practical life easier so that they may have the opportunity to practice the teachings which lead to spiritual evolution. The difference between an ordinary person and an enlightened Sage is that the Sage is never bound to the world, human emotions or the negative aspects of the mind (anger, frustration, hatred, greed, jealousy, etc.). He or she is always fulfilled, enjoying bliss and inner peace, no matter what may be occurring in the environment. A Sage is always in tune with nature. A Sage is always aware of his or her higher identity. He/she no longer identifies with the limited human ego, mind, and body, and therefore is not susceptible to depression or elation of any kind. A Sage sees the ego, the mind, and body as tools to carry out the divine work of the Creator, to guide souls to attain spiritual enlightenment.

Aset gains the power to bestow upon her son, Heru, the divine vision which is represented by the eyes of Ra. In this teaching, the left eye, the moon, symbolizes intellect or the relative knowledge of the Creation. The right eye represents the essence of the spirit. Both constitute a complementary whole of spiritual consciousness, spiritual enlightenment. This will help him succeed in the struggle to bring justice, truth, and righteousness to the world. This is the ideal for all human beings who follow the Goddess. They should see themselves as children of the Goddess. As they put themselves in her care by practicing the teachings of Yoga which she demonstrates through her myth and the disciplines of her temple, they will receive the fruits of spiritual wisdom, divine vision, immortality, and self-discovery or oneness with the Divine.

Thus, Aset is the healer of the greatest illness in all Creation. She heals human beings from the illness of ignorance of their true Self. She is the transmitter of the grace of the Divine to all Creation in the form of the eye of intuitional vision and in the form of her son Heru. Also, she is in possession of the power to assist every human being to survive the poison of ignorance and illusion about the world and about the nature of the Divine Self. This is what Aset meant when she referred to "a certain man, the son of a certain man," i.e., Asar (Osiris) and Heru (Horus), respectively. All spiritual aspirants are Asar and Heru. In the myth of the Ausarian Resurrection Aset resurrects both Heru and Asar through the power which comes from knowing the Divine Name of Ra.

The Self is the source and sustenance of all objects in creation from energy to atoms, from atoms to molecules, from molecules to compounds, from compounds to physical objects, plants, food, the human body, animals, planets, stars, etc.

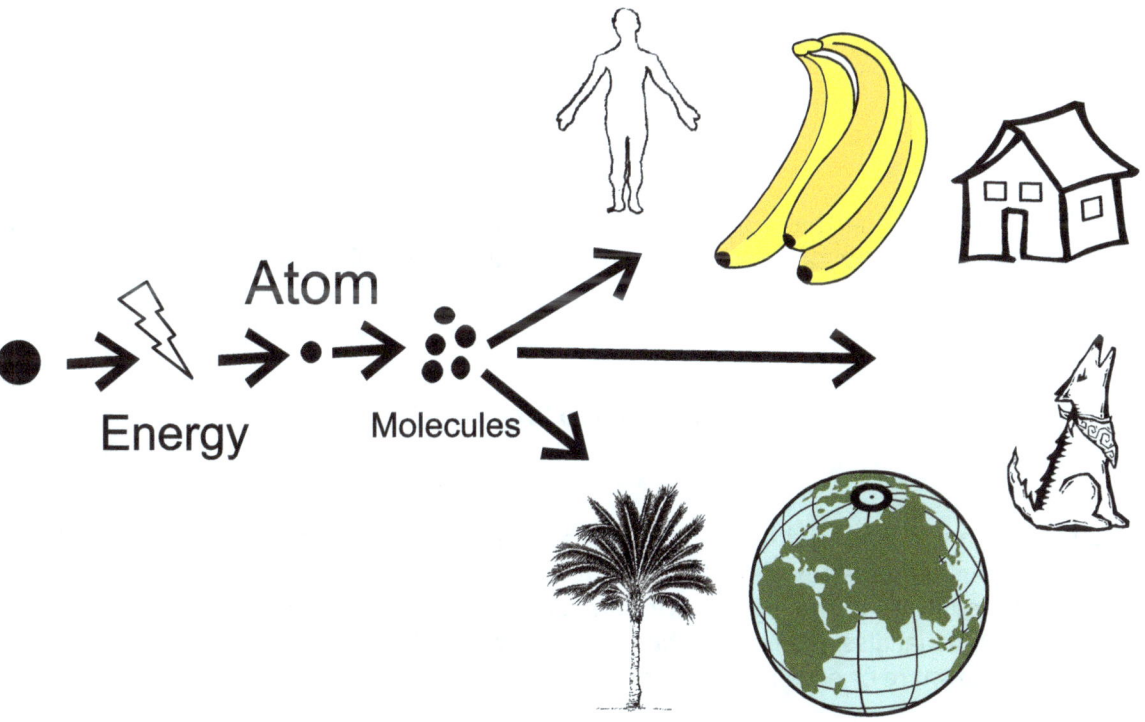

The goal of spiritual enlightenment based on the Story of Ra and Aset may be summarized as follows.

Worldly Knowledge is Lower Knowledge

A spiritual aspirant needs to become self-sufficient and capable of controlling his or her practical life. This means that a person should seek to learn the practical knowledge which will help them to survive in the practical world. Having done this the aspirant needs to always remember that worldly knowledge is lower knowledge. It is used to sustain the practical reality.

Aspiration

Aspiration is the awakening of the Spiritual Self, that is, becoming conscious of the divine presence within one's self and the universe by having faith that there is a spiritual essence beyond ordinary human understanding. It implies a desire to engage in spiritual study and self-discovery. Aspiration also means seeking after spiritual truth through the various disciplines known as Yoga.

Studying and Applying the Wisdom Teachings

Studying and applying the wisdom teachings implies practicing the teachings in day to day life. It means seeing beyond the opposites and understanding the underlying essence of Creation.

Inquiry Into Who Am I?

There is no more powerful question which a spiritual aspirant can ask other than "Who am I?" Everything in life depends on one's ego but if you ask the question, "Who am I?" it becomes clearer and clearer that the ego is not the real you, and everything that the ego wants is illusory. This spiritual discipline or practice allows a spiritual aspirant to gradually free himself or herself from the snare of egoism and ignorance.

Single-minded Determination To Know The Highest Truth

A spiritual aspirant cannot be satisfied with the intellectual understanding of "Who am I?" or nature of the Divine. There must be an overwhelming and one-pointed movement towards the ultimate goal, to experience the Divine.

Communion With The Divine

Aset was able to commune with Ra. This is how she obtained his real name. So too a spiritual aspirant must seek to commune with the Divine Self in order to attain enlightenment. This is accomplished by practicing all of the disciplines outlined here and through these, leading oneself into a transcendental state of consciousness which allows one to go beyond the ego and converse intimately with God. This is the ultimate goal which leads a person to become one with God.

OM HTP HTP HTP

Dr. Muata Ashby

INDEX

A

Ab, 93, 102
Absolute, 131, 133, 143
Actions, 23
Africa, 148, 154, 156, 157, 158
African Proverbial Wisdom Teachings, 162
African Religion, 2, 143, 149, 150, 153
Akhenaton, 100, 117
Alexandria, 8
Allopathic, 144
Amenta, 149
Amentet, 150
American Heritage Dictionary, Dictionary, 153
American Theocracy, 156
Amun, 76, 116
Ancient Egypt, 2, 8, 9, 16, 17, 18, 19, 20, 25, 28, 97, 110, 130, 131, 132, 143, 144, 145, 146, 147, 148, 149, 150, 151, 152, 153, 154, 155, 156, 157, 158, 160, 161, 162, 163, 164, 165, 167
Ancient Egyptian Mystery Religion, 110
Ancient Egyptian Wisdom Texts, 161
anger, 92, 132, 135, 136, 152
Ani, 9, 10
Ankh, 83, 96
Anu, 149
Anu (Greek Heliopolis), 149
Anunian Theology, 150
Apep serpent, 39
Aryan, 145
Asar, 22, 35, 54, 87, 89, 112, 117, 129, 136, 148, 149, 151
Asar and Aset, 148
Asarian Resurrection, 89, 91, 112, 118, 120, 148, 151, 152, 154
Aset, 1, 2, 7, 8, 12, 13, 14, 15, 26, 27, 28, 29, 30, 31, 35, 37, 41, 44, 61, 67, 74, 76, 77, 79, 81, 82, 83, 85, 86, 87, 89, 91, 93, 94, 98, 99, 105, 107, 109, 110, 111, 112, 113, 114, 115, 116, 117, 118, 119, 120, 121, 125, 126, 127, 128, 129, 130, 131, 132,133, 134, 135, 136, 137, 138, 146, 148, 149, 150, 151
Aset (Isis), 1, 2, 7, 8, 12, 13, 14, 15, 26, 27, 28, 29, 30, 31, 35, 37, 41, 44, 61, 67, 74, 76, 77, 79, 81, 82, 83, 85, 86, 87, 89, 91, 93, 94, 98, 99, 105, 107, 109, 110, 111, 112, 113, 114, 115, 116, 117, 118, 119, 120, 121, 125, 126, 127, 128, 129, 130, 131, 132,133, 134, 135, 136, 137, 138, 146, 148, 149, 150, 151
Ashanti, 162
Asia, 158
Asia Minor, 158
Asiatic, 156, 157, 158
Assyrians, 161
Astral, 131, 134, 149
Astral Plane, 131, 134, 149
Atlantis, 155
Aton, 100, 117
Awakening, 148, 166

B

Being, 54, 128, 129, 131, 135, 150
Bhagavad Gita, 161
Bible, 151
Black, 158
Black Africa, 158
Boat of Millions of Years, 29
Body, 165
Book of Coming Forth By Day, 149
Book of the Dead, see also Rau Nu Prt M Hru, 10, 11, 131, 149, 162
Brooklyn Museum, 99
Buddha, 154, 156, 168
Buddhism, 150, 156
Buddhist, 148, 156
Budge, Wallis, 10
Bull, 28, 69

C

Catholic, 151
Catholic Church, 151
Causal Plane, 131
Child, 151
Christ, 149
Christianity, 143, 150, 151
Church, 151
Civilization, 145, 156, 157, 158, 165
coercion, 157
Coffin Texts, 11
Collapse, 156, 165, 167
color, 8, 107, 160, 162
Color, 160
Conflict, 157, 163
Congress, 2
Consciousness, 90, 148, 162
Consciousness, human, 143
contentment, 167
Coptic, 10, 11, 148
cosmic force, 117, 150, 155
Creation, 27, 28, 35, 57, 58, 69, 77, 81, 91, 96, 102, 106, 107, 109, 114, 116, 117, 120, 126, 127, 129, 132, 133, 134, 135, 136, 138, 148, 149, 162
Culture, 147, 154, 159, 166

D

Death, 156, 165
December, 150
delusion, 81, 120
Denderah, 148
Desire, 163
Detachment, 86
Devotional Love, 146
Diet, 144
Dispassion, 86
Divine Word, 8
Dollar, U.S. Dollar, 167
Duality, 85
Duat, 149

E

Earth, 90, 113
Edfu, 148
Egyptian Book of Coming Forth By Day, 149
Egyptian Mysteries, 18, 144, 152, 153, 163, 164
Egyptian Physics, 150
Egyptian Proverb, 146
EGYPTIAN PROVERBS, 146
Egyptian Yoga, 143, 144, 148, 149

Egyptian Yoga see also Kamitan Yoga, 143, 144, 148, 149, 167, 168
Egyptologists, 8, 10, 11, 153, 160
Empire culture, 157
Energy, 131, 133
Enlightenment, 120, 124, 133, 143, 144, 146, 147, 148, 150, 152, 155, 163, 164, 165
ETHICS, 144, 145, 156, 157, 158, 162
Ethiopia, 162
Eucharist, 149
Europe, 7
evil, 152, 153
Evil, 154
Exercise, 148
Existence, 91
Eye, 29
Eye of Horus, 29

F

Face, 50
Faith, 158
faith-based, 120
Finances, 165
Fire, 83, 96
Flood, 69, 114
Form, 17
frustration, 132, 136

G

Galla, 162
Galla culture, 162
Geb, 148
Ghana, 162
global economy, 157
Globalization, 157
God, 21, 32, 36, 47, 51, 54, 79, 85, 90, 92, 117, 126, 131, 132, 133, 135, 138, 146, 149, 150, 154, 159
Goddess, 27, 31, 41, 86, 90, 92, 94, 127, 132, 136, 150, 159
Goddesses, 2, 58, 84, 85, 87, 90, 91, 92, 106, 109, 111, 114, 117, 121, 148, 153
Gods, 2, 36, 58, 84, 85, 87, 90, 91, 92, 106, 109, 111, 114, 117, 121, 148, 153
gods and goddesses, 27, 28, 29, 33, 36, 37, 39, 42, 47, 49, 52, 55, 60, 61, 70, 71, 77, 82, 85, 111, 114, 117, 131, 134, 149, 153, 155
Good, 154
Gospels, 151
Greece, 7, 144, 154
Greek philosophy, 143
Greeks, 161

H

Hapi, 29, 51, 71
Hate, 163
Hatha Yoga, 157
Hathor, 148, 150, 152, 168
Hatred, 163
Health, 143, 150
Heart, 104, 152, 159
Heart (also see Ab, mind, conscience), 104, 152, 159
Heaven, 83, 151
Heaven XE "Heaven" and Earth, 83
Hekau, 110, 167
Henotheism, 92
Hermes, 164
Hermes (see also Djehuti, Thoth), 164
Hermetic, 164
Hermeticism, 164
Heru, 29, 30, 35, 56, 70, 78, 79, 82, 83, 106, 110, 118, 119, 120, 121, 129, 135, 136, 148, 149, 150, 151, 154, 162
Heru (see Horus), 29, 30, 35, 56, 70, 78, 79, 82, 83, 106, 110, 118, 119, 120, 121, 129, 135, 136, 148, 149, 150, 151, 154, 162
Hetheru, 119, 152
Hetheru (Hetheru, Hathor), 119, 152
Hieratic, 8, 10, 11, 22
Hieroglyphic, 2, 10, 17, 18, 25, 147, 160, 164
Hieroglyphic Writing, language, 2, 10, 17, 18, 25, 147, 160, 164
Hieroglyphs, 8, 25
High God, 109
Hindu, 130
Hinduism, 150
Hindus, 153
hope, 159, 160
Horus, 29, 78, 79, 82, 110, 136
Humanity, 152
Hymn to Ra, 91, 98

I

Iamblichus, 161
illusion, 94, 95, 96, 106, 120, 132, 133, 134, 135, 136
Image, 10, 42, 97
Imhotep, 86
India, 144, 145, 147, 148, 156, 157
Indian Yoga, 145
Indus, 145
Indus Valley, 145
Initiate, 144
Isis, 7, 8, 27, 31, 37, 44, 61, 62, 67, 74, 76, 79, 81, 82, 86, 89, 98, 115, 116, 120, 121, 146, 148, 149, 150, 168
Isis and Osiris, see Asar and Aset, 8
Isis, See also Aset, 7, 8, 27, 31, 37, 44, 61, 62, 67, 74, 76, 79, 81, 82, 86, 89, 98, 115, 116, 120, 121, 146, 148, 149, 150, 168
Islam, 143

J

Jesus, 149, 151, 168
Jesus Christ, 149
Judaism, 143

K

Ka, 41, 94
Kabbalah, 143
Kamit (Egypt), 153
Kamitan, 144, 154
Karma, 147
Kemetic, 155, 159, 163, 165, 168
Khemn, see also ignorance, 153
Khepra, 72
Khepri, 97
Khufu, 105, 106
Khufu, see also Cheops, 105, 106
King, 85, 105, 106, 151, 154
Kingdom, 10, 11, 151
Kingdom of Heaven, 151
Knowledge, 86, 137
Krishna, 151
Kybalion, 164

L

Life, 80, 83, 86, 96, 119, 132, 133, 147, 154, 158, 159, 162
Life Force, 119, 132, 133, 147
Listening, 38, 86, 125
Love, 126, 146, 167
lucid, 96, 97

M

Maat, 92, 147, 150, 152, 155, 159, 162, 163, 164, 165
MAAT, 146
Maat Philosophy, 152, 155, 159, 164, 165
MAATI, 146
Malawi, 162

Matter, 131, 150
media, 157
Meditation, 38, 125, 126, 134, 144, 146, 147
Medu Neter, 153, 167
Memphite Theology, 150
Meskhenet, 147
Metaphysics, 150, 162
Middle East, 143
Middle Kingdom, 10, 11
Min, 148
Mind, 124, 133, 165
Modern physics, 131
Motion, 102
Music, 160
Mut, 110
Mysteries, 18, 27, 144, 152, 153, 161, 163, 164
mystical philosophy, 132, 156, 161
Mysticism, 145, 149, 150, 152, 156, 157, 158

N

Nature, 132
Neberdjer, 143
Nehast, 153
neo-con, 156
Neter, 1, 8, 9, 24, 32, 35, 41, 47, 49, 51, 54, 63, 67, 77, 79, 80, 81, 85, 87, 90, 94, 97, 113, 116, 117, 126, 146, 149, 153, 154, 156, 160, 163, 166, 167
Neterian, 8, 26, 38, 83, 110, 153, 154, 156, 166, 167, 168
Neterianism, 164, 166
Neteru, 36, 84, 90, 94, 117, 153
Netherworld, 124
New Kingdom, 10
Nigeria, 162
Nile River, 51, 89, 132
Nun (See also Nu primeval waters-unformed matter), 116
Nut, 97, 148

O

Ocean, 28, 129, 130, 134
Old age, 43
Old Kingdom, 10
One God, 92
Oneness, 85
Orion Star Constellation, 150
Orthodox, 153
Osiris, 8, 22, 54, 136, 148, 149, 154

P

Panentheistic, 106
Paraclete, 92, 109
Paut, 49
Peace, 163, 164, 166
Peace (see also Hetep), 163, 164, 166
Persians, 161
PERT EM HERU, SEE ALSO BOOK OF THE DEAD, 149
Pharaoh, 165
Philae, 7, 8, 148
Philosophy, 2, 18, 91, 143, 144, 145, 146, 149, 150, 152, 155, 156, 157, 158, 159, 164, 165
Physical, 131
Physical Plane, 131
physical world, 129
Plutarch, 8, 128
priests and priestesses, 10, 19, 27, 83, 127, 148, 154
Priests and Priestesses, 111, 144, 154
Primeval Waters, 116, 132
Proverbial Wisdom, 162
Psedjet (ennead), 129
Psychology, 150, 164
Ptah, 150
Ptahotep, 9

Q

quantum physics, 131
Queen, 154

R

Ra, 2, 8, 12, 13, 14, 15, 24, 26, 27, 28, 29, 31, 35, 40, 41, 42, 43, 44, 47, 48, 49, 50, 54, 57, 58, 61, 67, 70, 72, 73, 74, 76, 77, 78, 79, 81, 82, 83, 86, 89, 91, 92, 93, 94, 97, 98, 99, 101, 102, 105, 106, 107, 109, 110, 111, 113, 114, 115, 116, 117, 118, 119, 120, 121, 125, 127, 128, 129, 131, 132, 133, 134, 135, 136, 137, 138, 148
racism, 163
Racism, 163
Realization, 146
Reflection, 38, 125
relativity, 133, 135
Religion, 2, 143, 145, 149, 150, 151, 153, 154, 156, 157, 158, 166, 167
Ren, 41, 94, 97, 115, 116
Renaissance, 86
Resurrection, 129, 136, 148, 149, 150, 151, 152, 154
RITUAL, 152
Rituals, 150
Roman, 161
Romans, 161
Rome, 155

S

Saa (spiritual understanding faculty), 86, 92
Sages, 124, 131, 143, 148, 149, 152, 155, 168
Saints, 149, 168
School, 9
Sebai, 27, 89, 95, 96, 98, 124, 125, 126, 127, 155, 159, 164, 166
See also Ra-Hrakti, 2, 8, 12, 13, 14, 15, 24, 26, 27, 28, 29, 31, 35, 40, 41, 42, 43, 44, 47, 48, 49, 50, 54, 57, 58, 61, 67, 70, 72, 73, 74, 76, 77, 78, 79, 81, 82, 83, 86, 89, 91, 92, 93, 94, 97, 98, 99, 101, 102, 105, 106, 107, 109, 110, 111, 113, 114, 115, 116, 117, 118, 119, 120, 121, 125, 127, 128, 129, 131, 132, 133, 134, 135, 136, 137, 138, 148
Sekhem, 93
Sekhemit, 35
Self (see Ba, soul, Spirit, Universal, Ba, Neter, Heru)., 54, 91, 116, 117, 120, 131, 133, 135, 136, 137, 138, 145, 146, 147, 148, 152, 159
Self (seeBasoulSpiritUniversal BaNeterHorus)., 133, 135, 136, 137, 138
Sema, 1, 2, 30, 154, 163, 165, 167
Sema Tawi, 167
Serpent, 48, 93, 101, 107, 132, 133
Serpent Power, 93, 101, 132, 133
Serpent Power (see also Kundalini and Buto), 93, 101, 132, 133
Serpent Power see also Kundalini Yoga, 93, 101, 132, 133
Set, 89, 118, 154
Seti I, 147
Setian, 91, 101
Sex, 148
sexism, 163
Sexism, 163
Shedy, 144
Sheps, 90, 97
Shetaut Neter, 1, 85, 91, 149, 153, 154, 156, 163, 166, 167

Shetaut Neter See also Egyptian Religion, 1, 85, 91, 149, 153, 154, 156, 163, 166, 167
Sirius, 150
skin, 24, 43, 101
slavery, 153
Snake, 62
Snake (also see serpent), 62
society, 144, 153, 155, 159, 162, 163, 165, 167
Society, 164, 165, 167
Soul, 154, 165
Spirit, 124, 125
Spiritual discipline, 144
SPIRITUALITY, 144, 159, 166, 168
Studying, 138
Sublimation, 148
Sunrays, 99
Superpower, 156
Superpower Syndrome, 157
Superpower Syndrome Mandatory Conflict Complex, 157
Supreme Being, 54, 92, 129, 131, 135, 150
Supreme Divinity, 27

T

TANTRA, 148
TANTRA YOGA, 148
Tao, 91
Taoism, 143
Tawi, 167
Television, 90, 102
Tem, 43, 44, 77, 97, 98, 107, 118

Temple, 1, 7, 8, 26, 27, 93, 102, 127, 148, 152, 166
Temple of Aset, 1, 7, 8, 26, 27, 102, 127, 148
Temu, 29, 31, 32, 56, 73, 82, 110, 114, 121
The Absolute, 143
The Black, 158
The God, 51, 109, 148
The Gods, 109, 148
The Self, 131, 133, 136
Theban Theology, 143
Thebes, 143, 147
Theocracy, 156
Theology, 143, 150
time and space, 35, 85, 90, 94, 95, 96, 105, 110, 113, 117, 119, 120, 124, 125, 129, 132, 133, 134, 135, 153
Tomb, 147
Tomb of Seti I, 147
Tradition, 117
transcendental reality, 135, 153
Tree, 162
Tree of Life, 162
Triad, 143
Trinity, 129, 149
Trinity of Asar XE "Asar" , Aset XE "Aset" and Heru, 129
Truth, 138

U

Understanding, 86, 153, 164
United States of America, 156

Universal Consciousness, 148
Upanishads, 149, 161

V

Vedanta, 91
Vedic, 145
Violence, 163

W

Waset, 143
Wealth, Money, 165
White, 165
Who am I, 132, 138
Wisdom, 93, 134, 138, 146, 147, 161, 162, 165
Wisdom (also see Djehuti), 134, 138
Wisdom (also see Djehuti, Aset), 93, 134, 138, 146, 147, 161, 162, 165
World War II, 157

Y

Yoga, 2, 132, 134, 136, 137, 143, 144, 145, 148, 149, 150, 152, 154, 156, 157, 158, 167, 168
Yoga of Devotion (see Yoga of Divine Love), 167
Yoga of Wisdom (see also Jnana Yoga), 134
Yogic, 157, 163
Yoruba, 162

Other Books From C M Books

P.O.Box 570459

Miami, Florida, 33257

(305) 378-6253 Fax: (305) 378-6253

Prices subject to change.

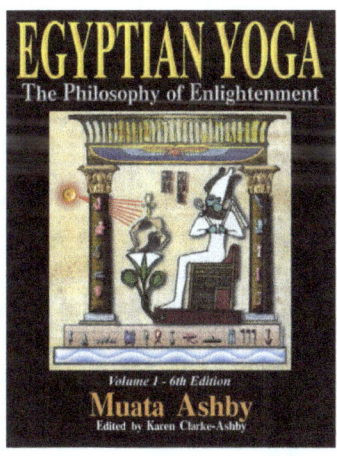

1. *EGYPTIAN YOGA: THE PHILOSOPHY OF ENLIGHTENMENT* An original, fully illustrated work, including hieroglyphs, detailing the meaning of the Egyptian mysteries, tantric yoga, psycho-spiritual and physical exercises. Egyptian Yoga is a guide to the practice of the highest spiritual philosophy which leads to absolute freedom from human misery and to immortality. It is well known by scholars that Egyptian philosophy is the basis of Western and Middle Eastern religious philosophies such as *Christianity, Islam, Judaism,* the *Kabala*, and Greek philosophy, but what about Indian philosophy, Yoga and Taoism? What were the original teachings? How can they be practiced today? What is the source of pain and suffering in the world and what is the solution? Discover the deepest mysteries of the mind and universe within and outside of yourself. 8.5" X 11" ISBN: 1-884564-01-1 Soft $19.95

2. *EGYPTIAN YOGA: African Religion Volume 2*- Theban Theology U.S. In this long awaited sequel to *Egyptian Yoga: The Philosophy of Enlightenment* you will take a fascinating and enlightening journey back in time and discover the teachings which constituted the epitome of Ancient Egyptian spiritual wisdom. What are the disciplines which lead to the fulfillment of all desires? Delve into the three states of consciousness (waking, dream and deep sleep) and the fourth state which transcends them all, Neberdjer, "The Absolute." These teachings of the city of Waset (Thebes) were the crowning achievement of the Sages of Ancient Egypt. They establish the standard mystical keys for understanding the profound mystical symbolism of the Triad of human consciousness. ISBN 1-884564-39-9 $23.95

3. *THE KEMETIC DIET: GUIDE TO HEALTH, DIET AND FASTING* Health issues have always been important to human beings since the beginning of time. The earliest records of history show that the art of healing was held in high esteem since the time of Ancient Egypt. In the early 20th century, medical doctors had almost attained the status of sainthood by the promotion of the idea that they alone were "scientists" while other healing modalities and traditional healers who did not follow the "scientific method' were nothing but superstitious, ignorant charlatans who at best would take the money of their clients and at worst kill them with the

unscientific "snake oils" and "irrational theories". In the late 20th century, the failure of the modern medical establishment's ability to lead the general public to good health, promoted the move by many in society towards "alternative medicine". Alternative medicine disciplines are those healing modalities which do not adhere to the philosophy of allopathic medicine. Allopathic medicine is what medical doctors practice by an large. It is the theory that disease is caused by agencies outside the body such as bacteria, viruses or physical means which affect the body. These can therefore be treated by medicines and therapies The natural healing method began in the absence of extensive technologies with the idea that all the answers for health may be found in nature or rather, the deviation from nature. Therefore, the health of the body can be restored by correcting the aberration and thereby restoring balance. This is the area that will be covered in this volume. Allopathic techniques have their place in the art of healing. However, we should not forget that the body is a grand achievement of the spirit and built into it is the capacity to maintain itself and heal itself. Ashby, Muata   ISBN: 1-884564-49-6 $28.95

4. INITIATION INTO EGYPTIAN YOGA Shedy: Spiritual discipline or program, to go deeply into the mysteries, to study the mystery teachings and literature profoundly, to penetrate the mysteries. You will learn about the mysteries of initiation into the teachings and practice of Yoga and how to become an Initiate of the mystical sciences. This insightful manual is the first in a series which introduces you to the goals of daily spiritual and yoga practices: Meditation, Diet, Words of Power and the ancient wisdom teachings. 8.5" X 11" ISBN 1-884564-02-X Soft Cover $24.95 U.S.

5. *THE AFRICAN ORIGINS OF CIVILIZATION, RELIGION AND YOGA SPIRITUALITY AND ETHICS PHILOSOPHY* HARD COVER EDITION Part 1, Part 2, Part 3 in one volume 683 Pages Hard Cover First Edition Three volumes in one. Over the past several years I have been asked to put together in one volume the most important evidences showing the correlations and common teachings between Kamitan (Ancient Egyptian) culture and religion and that of India. The questions of the history of Ancient Egypt, and the latest archeological evidences showing civilization and culture in Ancient Egypt and its spread to other countries, has intrigued many scholars as well as mystics over the years. Also, the possibility that Ancient Egyptian Priests and Priestesses migrated to Greece, India and other countries to carry on the traditions of the Ancient Egyptian Mysteries, has been speculated over the years as well. In chapter 1 of the book *Egyptian Yoga The Philosophy of Enlightenment,* 1995, I first introduced the deepest comparison between Ancient Egypt and India that had been brought forth up to that time. Now, in the year 2001 this new book,

THE AFRICAN ORIGINS OF CIVILIZATION, MYSTICAL RELIGION AND YOGA PHILOSOPHY, more fully explores the motifs, symbols and philosophical correlations between Ancient Egyptian and Indian mysticism and clearly shows not only that Ancient Egypt and India were connected culturally but also spiritually. How does this knowledge help the spiritual aspirant? This discovery has great importance for the Yogis and mystics who follow the philosophy of Ancient Egypt and the mysticism of India. It means that India has a longer history and heritage than was previously understood. It shows that the mysteries of Ancient Egypt were essentially a yoga tradition which did not die but rather developed into the modern day systems of Yoga technology of India. It further shows that African culture developed Yoga Mysticism earlier than any other civilization in history. All of this expands our understanding of the unity of culture and the deep legacy of Yoga, which stretches into the distant past, beyond the Indus Valley civilization, the earliest known high culture in India as well as the Vedic tradition of Aryan culture. Therefore, Yoga culture and mysticism is the oldest known tradition of spiritual development and Indian mysticism is an extension of the Ancient Egyptian mysticism. By understanding the legacy which Ancient Egypt gave to India the mysticism of India is better understood and by comprehending the heritage of Indian Yoga, which is rooted in Ancient Egypt the Mysticism of Ancient Egypt is also better understood. This expanded understanding allows us to prove the underlying kinship of humanity, through the common symbols, motifs and philosophies which are not disparate and confusing teachings but in reality expressions of the same study of truth through metaphysics and mystical realization of Self. (HARD COVER)

ISBN: 1-884564-50-X $45.00 U.S. 8 1/2" X 11"

6. *AFRICAN ORIGINS BOOK 1 PART 1* African Origins of African Civilization, Religion, Yoga Mysticism and Ethics Philosophy-Soft Cover $24.95 ISBN: 1-884564-55-0

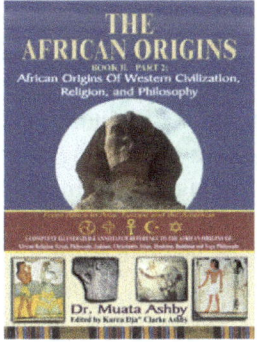

7. *AFRICAN ORIGINS BOOK 2 PART 2* African Origins of Western Civilization, Religion and Philosophy (Soft) -Soft Cover $24.95 ISBN: 1-884564-56-9

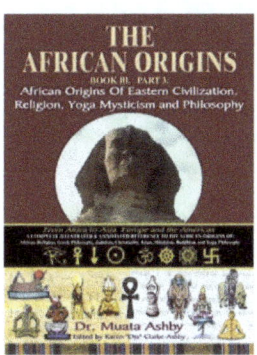

8. *EGYPT AND INDIA AFRICAN ORIGINS OF Eastern Civilization, Religion, Yoga Mysticism and Philosophy*-Soft Cover $29.95 (Soft) ISBN: 1-884564-57-7

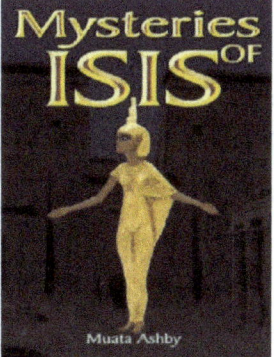

9. *THE MYSTERIES OF ISIS: **The Ancient Egyptian Philosophy of Self-Realization*** - There are several paths to discover the Divine and the mysteries of the higher Self. This volume details the mystery teachings of the goddess Aset (Isis) from Ancient Egypt- the path of wisdom. It includes the teachings of her temple and the disciplines that are enjoined for the initiates of the temple of Aset as they were given in ancient times. Also, this book includes the teachings of the main myths of Aset that lead a human being to spiritual enlightenment and immortality. Through the study of ancient myth and the illumination of initiatic understanding the idea of God is expanded from the mythological comprehension to the metaphysical. Then this metaphysical understanding is related to you, the student, so as to begin understanding your true divine nature. ISBN 1-884564-24-0 $22.99

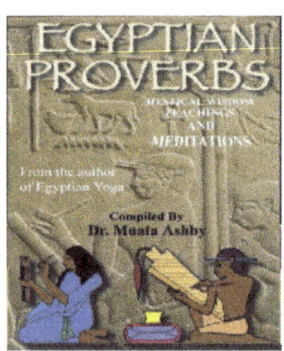

10. *EGYPTIAN PROVERBS:* collection of —Ancient Egyptian Proverbs and Wisdom Teachings -How to live according to MAAT Philosophy. Beginning Meditation. All proverbs are indexed for easy searches. For the first time in one volume, ——Ancient Egyptian Proverbs, wisdom teachings and meditations, fully illustrated with hieroglyphic text and symbols. EGYPTIAN PROVERBS is a unique collection of knowledge and wisdom which you can put into practice today and transform your life. $14.95 U'S ISBN: 1-884564-00-3

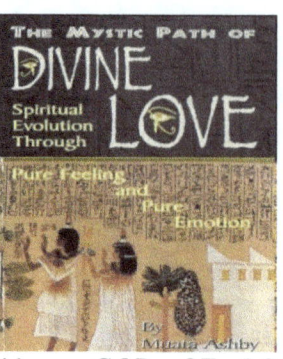

11. *GOD OF LOVE: THE PATH OF DIVINE LOVE The Process of Mystical Transformation and The Path of Divine Love* This Volume focuses on the ancient wisdom teachings of "Neter Merri" –the Ancient Egyptian philosophy of Divine Love and how to use them in a scientific process for self-transformation. Love is one of the most powerful human emotions. It is also the source of Divine feeling that unifies God and the individual human being. When love is fragmented and diminished by egoism the Divine connection is lost. The Ancient tradition of Neter Merri leads human beings back to their Divine connection, allowing them to discover their innate glorious self that is actually Divine and immortal. This volume will detail the process of transformation from ordinary consciousness to cosmic consciousness through the integrated practice of the teachings and the path of Devotional Love toward the Divine. 5.5"x 8.5" ISBN 1-884564-11-9 $22.95

12. *INTRODUCTION TO MAAT PHILOSOPHY: Spiritual Enlightenment Through the Path of Virtue* Known

commonly as Karma in India, the teachings of MAAT contain an extensive philosophy based on ariu (deeds) and their fructification in the form of shai and renenet (fortune and destiny, leading to Meskhenet (fate in a future birth) for living virtuously and with orderly wisdom are explained and the student is to begin practicing the precepts of Maat in daily life so as to promote the process of purification of the heart in preparation for the judgment of the soul. This judgment will be understood not as an event that will occur at the time of death but as an event that occurs continuously, at every moment in the life of the individual. The student will learn how to become allied with the forces of the Higher Self and to thereby begin cleansing the mind (heart) of impurities so as to attain a higher vision of reality. ISBN 1-884564-20-8 $22.99

13. *MEDITATION The Ancient Egyptian Path to Enlightenment* Many people do not know about the rich history of meditation practice in Ancient Egypt. This volume outlines the theory of meditation and presents the Ancient Egyptian Hieroglyphic text which give instruction as to the nature of the mind and its three modes of expression. It also presents the texts which give instruction on the practice of meditation for spiritual Enlightenment and unity with the Divine. This volume allows the reader to begin practicing meditation by explaining, in easy to understand terms, the simplest form of meditation and working up to the most advanced form which was practiced in ancient times and which is still practiced by yogis around the world in modern times. ISBN 1-884564-27-7 $22.99

14. *THE GLORIOUS LIGHT MEDITATION* TECHNIQUE OF ANCIENT EGYPT New for the year 2000. This volume is based on the earliest known instruction in history given for the practice of formal meditation. Discovered by Dr. Muata Ashby, it is inscribed on the walls of the Tomb of Seti I in Thebes Egypt. This volume details the philosophy and practice of this unique system of meditation originated in Ancient Egypt and the earliest practice of meditation known in the world which occurred in the most advanced African Culture. ISBN: 1-884564-15-1 $16.95 (PB)

15. *THE SERPENT POWER: The Ancient Egyptian Mystical Wisdom of the Inner Life Force.* This Volume specifically deals with the latent life Force energy of the universe and in the human body, its control and sublimation. How to develop the Life Force energy of the subtle body. This Volume will introduce

the esoteric wisdom of the science of how virtuous living acts in a subtle and mysterious way to cleanse the latent psychic energy conduits and vortices of the spiritual body. ISBN 1-884564-19-4 $22.95

16. EGYPTIAN YOGA *The Postures of The Gods and Goddesses* Discover the physical postures and exercises practiced thousands of years ago in Ancient Egypt which are today known as Yoga exercises. Discover the history of the postures and how they were transferred from Ancient Egypt in Africa to India through Buddhist Tantrism. Then practice the postures as you discover the mythic teaching that originally gave birth to the postures and was practiced by the Ancient Egyptian priests and priestesses. This work is based on the pictures and teachings from the Creation story of Ra, The Asarian Resurrection Myth and the carvings and reliefs from various Temples in Ancient Egypt 8.5" X 11" ISBN 1-884564-10-0 Soft Cover $21.95   Exercise video $20

17. SACRED SEXUALITY: ANCIENT EGYPTIAN TANTRA YOGA: *The Art of Sex* Sublimation and Universal Consciousness This Volume will expand on the male and female principles within the human body and in the universe and further detail the sublimation of sexual energy into spiritual energy. The student will study the deities Min and Hathor, Asar and Aset, Geb and Nut and discover the mystical implications for a practical spiritual discipline. This Volume will also focus on the Tantric aspects of Ancient Egyptian and Indian mysticism, the purpose of sex and the mystical teachings of sexual sublimation which lead to self-knowledge and Enlightenment.   ISBN 1-884564-03-8 $24.95

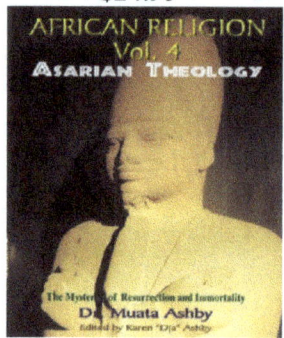

18. AFRICAN RELIGION Volume 4: ASARIAN THEOLOGY: RESURRECTING OSIRIS The path of Mystical Awakening and the Keys to Immortality NEW REVISED AND EXPANDED EDITION! The Ancient Sages created stories based on human and superhuman beings whose struggles, aspirations, needs and desires ultimately lead them to discover their true Self. The myth of Aset, Asar and Heru is no exception in this area. While there is no one source where the entire story may be found, pieces of it are inscribed in various ancient Temples walls, tombs, steles and papyri. For the first time available, the complete myth of Asar, Aset and Heru has been compiled from original Ancient Egyptian, Greek and Coptic Texts. This epic myth has been richly illustrated with reliefs from the Temple of Heru at Edfu, the Temple of Aset at Philae, the Temple of Asar at Abydos, the Temple of Hathor at Denderah and various papyri, inscriptions and reliefs. Discover the

myth which inspired the teachings of the *Shetaut Neter* (Egyptian Mystery System - Egyptian Yoga) and the Egyptian Book of Coming Forth By Day. Also, discover the three levels of Ancient Egyptian Religion, how to understand the mysteries of the Duat or Astral World and how to discover the abode of the Supreme in the Amenta, *The Other World* The ancient religion of Asar, Aset and Heru, if properly understood, contains all of the elements necessary to lead the sincere aspirant to attain immortality through inner self-discovery. This volume presents the entire myth and explores the main mystical themes and rituals associated with the myth for understating human existence, creation and the way to achieve spiritual emancipation - *Resurrection.* The Asarian myth is so powerful that it influenced and is still having an effect on the major world religions. Discover the origins and mystical meaning of the Christian Trinity, the Eucharist ritual and the ancient origin of the birthday of Jesus Christ. Soft Cover ISBN: 1-884564-27-5 $24.95

hieroglyphic scripture over 150 years ago. The astonishing writings in it reveal that the Ancient Egyptians believed in life after death and in an ultimate destiny to discover the Divine. The elegance and aesthetic beauty of the hieroglyphic text itself has inspired many see it as an art form in and of itself. But is there more to it than that? Did the Ancient Egyptian wisdom contain more than just aphorisms and hopes of eternal life beyond death? In this volume Dr. Muata Ashby, the author of over 25 books on Ancient Egyptian Yoga Philosophy has produced a new translation of the original texts which uncovers a mystical teaching underlying the sayings and rituals instituted by the Ancient Egyptian Sages and Saints. "Once the philosophy of Ancient Egypt is understood as a mystical tradition instead of as a religion or primitive mythology, it reveals its secrets which if practiced today will lead anyone to discover the glory of spiritual self-discovery. The Pert em Heru is in every way comparable to the Indian Upanishads or the Tibetan Book of the Dead." $28.95 ISBN# 1-884564-28-3 Size: 8½" X 11

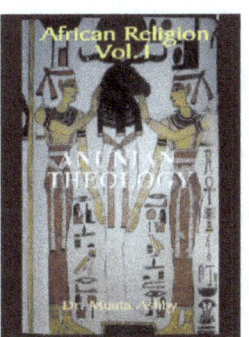

19. *THE EGYPTIAN BOOK OF THE DEAD MYSTICISM OF THE PERT EM HERU* " I Know myself, I know myself, I am One With God!–From the Pert Em Heru "The Ru Pert em Heru" or "Ancient Egyptian Book of The Dead," or "Book of Coming Forth By Day" as it is more popularly known, has fascinated the world since the successful translation of Ancient Egyptian

20. *African Religion VOL. 1- ANUNIAN THEOLOGY THE MYSTERIES OF RA* The Philosophy of Anu and The Mystical Teachings of The Ancient Egyptian Creation Myth Discover the mystical teachings contained in the Creation Myth and the gods and goddesses who brought creation and human beings into existence. The Creation myth of Anu is the source of

Anunian Theology but also of the other main theological systems of Ancient Egypt that also influenced other world religions including Christianity, Hinduism and Buddhism. The Creation Myth holds the key to understanding the universe and for attaining spiritual Enlightenment. ISBN: 1-884564-38-0 $19.95

21. *African Religion VOL 3: Memphite Theology: MYSTERIES OF MIND* Mystical Psychology & Mental Health for Enlightenment and Immortality based on the Ancient Egyptian Philosophy of Menefer -Mysticism of Ptah, Egyptian Physics and Yoga Metaphysics and the Hidden properties of Matter. This volume uncovers the mystical psychology of the Ancient Egyptian wisdom teachings centering on the philosophy of the Ancient Egyptian city of Menefer (Memphite Theology). How to understand the mind and how to control the senses and lead the mind to health, clarity and mystical self-discovery. This Volume will also go deeper into the philosophy of God as creation and will explore the concepts of modern science and how they correlate with ancient teachings. This Volume will lay the ground work for the understanding of the philosophy of universal consciousness and the initiatic/yogic insight into who or what is God? ISBN 1-884564-07-0 $22.95

22. *AFRICAN RELIGION VOLUME 5: THE GODDESS AND THE EGYPTIAN MYSTERIESTHE PATH OF THE GODDESS THE GODDESS PATH* The Secret Forms of the Goddess and the Rituals of Resurrection The Supreme Being may be worshipped as father or as mother. *Ushet Rekhat* or *Mother Worship*, is the spiritual process of worshipping the Divine in the form of the Divine Goddess. It celebrates the most important forms of the Goddess including *Nathor, Maat, Aset, Arat, Amentet and Hathor* and explores their mystical meaning as well as the rising of *Sirius,* the star of Aset (Aset) and the new birth of Hor (Heru). The end of the year is a time of reckoning, reflection and engendering a new or renewed positive movement toward attaining spiritual Enlightenment. The Mother Worship devotional meditation ritual, performed on five days during the month of December and on New Year's Eve, is based on the Ushet Rekhit. During the ceremony, the cosmic forces, symbolized by Sirius - and the constellation of Orion ---, are harnessed through the understanding and devotional attitude of the participant. This propitiation draws the light of wisdom and health to all those who share in the ritual, leading to prosperity and wisdom. $14.95 ISBN 1-884564-18-6

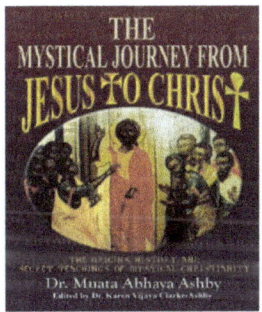

23. **THE MYSTICAL JOURNEY FROM JESUS TO CHRIST** Discover the ancient Egyptian origins of Christianity before the Catholic Church and learn the mystical teachings given by Jesus to assist all humanity in becoming Christlike. Discover the secret meaning of the Gospels that were discovered in Egypt. Also discover how and why so many Christian churches came into being. Discover that the Bible still holds the keys to mystical realization even though its original writings were changed by the church. Discover how to practice the original teachings of Christianity which leads to the Kingdom of Heaven. $24.95 ISBN# 1-884564-05-4 size: 8½" X 11"

24. **THE STORY OF ASAR, ASET AND HERU:** An Ancient Egyptian Legend (For Children) Now for the first time, the most ancient myth of Ancient Egypt comes alive for children. Inspired by the books *The Asarian Resurrection: The Ancient Egyptian Bible* and *The Mystical Teachings of The Asarian Resurrection*, *The Story of Asar, Aset and Heru* is an easy to understand and thrilling tale which inspired the children of Ancient Egypt to aspire to greatness and righteousness. If you and your child have enjoyed stories like *The Lion King* and *Star Wars* you will love *The Story of Asar, Aset and Heru.* Also, if you know the story of Jesus and Krishna you will discover than Ancient Egypt had a similar myth and that this myth carries important spiritual teachings for living a fruitful and fulfilling life. This book may be used along with *The Parents Guide To The Asarian Resurrection Myth: How to Teach Yourself and Your Child the Principles of Universal Mystical Religion.* The guide provides some background to the Asarian Resurrection myth and it also gives insight into the mystical teachings contained in it which you may introduce to your child. It is designed for parents who wish to grow spiritually with their children and it serves as an introduction for those who would like to study the Asarian Resurrection Myth in depth and to practice its teachings. 8.5" X 11" ISBN: 1-884564-31-3 $12.95

25. **THE PARENTS GUIDE TO THE AUSARIAN RESURRECTION MYTH:** How to Teach Yourself and Your Child the Principles of Universal Mystical Religion. This insightful manual brings for the timeless wisdom of the ancient through the Ancient Egyptian myth of Asar, Aset and Heru and the mystical teachings contained in it for parents who want to guide their children to understand and practice the teachings of mystical spirituality. This manual may be used with the children's storybook *The Story of Asar, Aset and*

Heru by Dr. Muata Abhaya Ashby.
ISBN: 1-884564-30-5 $16.95

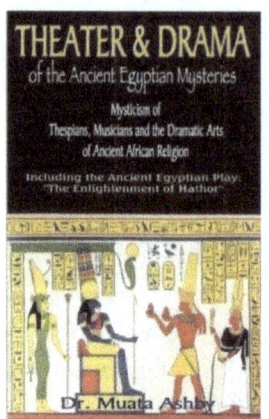

26. **HEALING THE CRIMINAL HEART.** Introduction to Maat Philosophy, Yoga and Spiritual Redemption Through the Path of Virtue   Who is a criminal? Is there such a thing as a criminal heart? What is the source of evil and sinfulness and is there any way to rise above it? Is there redemption for those who have committed sins, even the worst crimes? Ancient Egyptian mystical psychology holds important answers to these questions. Over ten thousand years ago mystical psychologists, the Sages of Ancient Egypt, studied and charted the human mind and spirit and laid out a path which will lead to spiritual redemption, prosperity and Enlightenment.   This introductory volume brings forth the teachings of the Asarian Resurrection, the most important myth of Ancient Egypt, with relation to the faults of human existence: anger, hatred, greed, lust, animosity, discontent, ignorance, egoism jealousy, bitterness, and a myriad of psycho-spiritual ailments which keep a human being in a state of negativity and adversity   ISBN: 1-884564-17-8 $15.95

27. *TEMPLE RITUAL OF THE ANCIENT EGYPTIAN MYSTERIES--THEATER & DRAMA OF THE ANCIENT EGYPTIAN MYSTERIES*: Details the practice of the mysteries and ritual program of the temple and the philosophy an practice of the ritual of the mysteries, its purpose and execution. Featuring the Ancient Egyptian stage play-"The Enlightenment of Hathor' Based on an Ancient Egyptian Drama, The original Theater -Mysticism of the Temple of Hetheru 1-884564-14-3 $19.95 By Dr. Muata Ashby

28. *GUIDE TO PRINT ON DEMAND: SELF-PUBLISH FOR PROFIT, SPIRITUAL FULFILLMENT AND SERVICE TO HUMANITY* Everyone asks us how we produced so many books in such a short time. Here are the secrets to writing and producing books that uplift humanity and how to get them printed for a fraction of the regular cost. Anyone can become an author even if they have limited funds. All that is necessary is the willingness to learn how the printing and book business work and the desire

to follow the special instructions given here for preparing your manuscript format. Then you take your work directly to the non-traditional companies who can produce your books for less than the traditional book printer can. ISBN: 1-884564-40-2 $16.95 U. S.

29. *Egyptian Mysteries: Vol. 1,* Shetaut Neter What are the Mysteries? For thousands of years the spiritual tradition of Ancient Egypt, S*hetaut Neter,* "The Egyptian Mysteries," "The Secret Teachings," have fascinated, tantalized and amazed the world. At one time exalted and recognized as the highest culture of the world, by Africans, Europeans, Asiatics, Hindus, Buddhists and other cultures of the ancient world, in time it was shunned by the emerging orthodox world religions. Its temples desecrated, its philosophy maligned, its tradition spurned, its philosophy dormant in the mystical *Medu Neter*, the mysterious hieroglyphic texts which hold the secret symbolic meaning that has scarcely been discerned up to now. What are the secrets of *Nehast* {spiritual awakening and emancipation, resurrection}. More than just a literal translation, this volume is for awakening to the secret code *Shetitu* of the teaching which was not deciphered by Egyptologists, nor could be understood by ordinary spiritualists. This book is a reinstatement of the original science made available for our times, to the reincarnated followers of Ancient Egyptian culture and the prospect of spiritual freedom to break the bonds of *Khemn,* "ignorance," and slavery to evil forces: *Såaa* . ISBN: 1-884564-41-0 $19.99

30. *EGYPTIAN MYSTERIES VOL 2:* Dictionary of Gods and Goddesses This book is about the mystery of neteru, the gods and goddesses of Ancient Egypt (Kamit, Kemet). Neteru means "Gods and Goddesses." But the Neterian teaching of Neteru represents more than the usual limited modern day concept of "divinities" or "spirits." The Neteru of Kamit are also metaphors, cosmic principles and vehicles for the enlightening teachings of Shetaut Neter (Ancient Egyptian-African Religion). Actually they are the elements for one of the most advanced systems of spirituality ever conceived in human history. Understanding the concept of neteru provides a firm basis for spiritual evolution and the pathway for viable culture, peace on earth and a healthy human society.   Why is it important to have gods and goddesses in our lives? In order for spiritual evolution to be possible, once a human being has accepted that there is existence after death and there is a transcendental being who exists beyond time and space knowledge, human beings need a connection to that which transcends the ordinary experience of human life in time and space and a means to understand the transcendental reality beyond the mundane reality. ISBN: 1-884564-23-2 $21.95

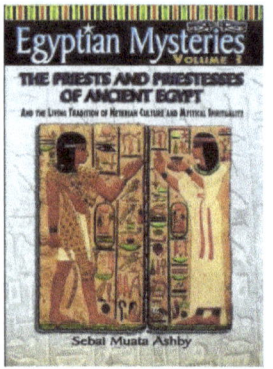

31. *EGYPTIAN MYSTERIES VOL. 3* The Priests and Priestesses of Ancient Egypt This volume details the path of Neterian priesthood, the joys, challenges and rewards of advanced Neterian life, the teachings that allowed the priests and priestesses to manage the most long lived civilization in human history and how that path can be adopted today; for those who want to tread the path of the Clergy of Shetaut Neter. ISBN: 1-884564-53-4 $24.95

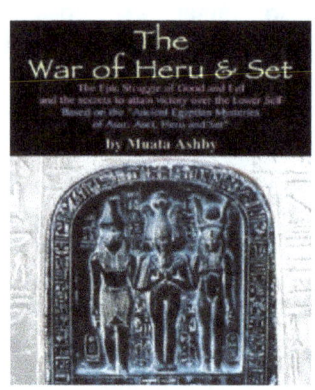

32. *The War of Heru and Set:* The Struggle of Good and Evil for Control of the World and The Human Soul This volume contains a novelized version of the Asarian Resurrection myth that is based on the actual scriptures presented in the Book Asarian Religion (old name –Resurrecting Osiris). This volume is prepared in the form of a screenplay and can be easily adapted to be used as a stage play. Spiritual seeking is a mythic journey that has many emotional highs and lows, ecstasies and depressions, victories and frustrations. This is the War of Life that is played out in the myth as the struggle of Heru and Set and those are mythic characters that represent the human Higher and Lower self. How to understand the war and emerge victorious in the journey of life? The ultimate victory and fulfillment can be experienced, which is not changeable or lost in time. The purpose of myth is to convey the wisdom of life through the story of divinities who show the way to overcome the challenges and foibles of life. In this volume the feelings and emotions of the characters of the myth have been highlighted to show the deeply rich texture of the Ancient Egyptian myth. This myth contains deep spiritual teachings and insights into the nature of self, of God and the mysteries of life and the means to discover the true meaning of life and thereby achieve the true purpose of life. To become victorious in the battle of life means to become the King (or Queen) of Egypt. Have you seen movies like The Lion King, Hamlet, The Odyssey, or The Little Buddha? These have been some of the most popular movies in modern times. The Sema Institute of Yoga is dedicated to researching and presenting the wisdom and culture of ancient Africa. The Script is designed to be produced as a motion picture but may be addapted for the theater as well. $21.95 copyright 1998 By Dr. Muata Ashby ISBN 1-8840564-44-5

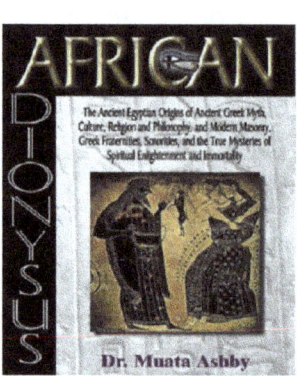

33. *AFRICAN DIONYSUS: FROM EGYPT TO GREECE:* The Kamitan Origins of Greek Culture and Religion ISBN: 1-

884564-47-X FROM EGYPT TO GREECE
This insightful manual is a reference to Ancient Egyptian mythology and philosophy and its correlation to what later became known as Greek and Rome mythology and philosophy. It outlines the basic tenets of the mythologies and shoes the ancient origins of Greek culture in Ancient Egypt. This volume also documents the origins of the Greek alphabet in Egypt as well as Greek religion, myth and philosophy of the gods and goddesses from Egypt from the myth of Atlantis and archaic period with the Minoans to the Classical period. This volume also acts as a resource for Colleges students who would like to set up fraternities and sororities based on the original Ancient Egyptian principles of Sheti and Maat philosophy. ISBN: 1-884564-47-X $22.95 U.S.

philosophy was the basis of Ancient Egyptian society and government as well as the heart of Ancient Egyptian myth and spirituality. Maat is at once a goddess, a cosmic force and a living social doctrine, which promotes social harmony and thereby paves the way for spiritual evolution in all levels of society. ISBN: 1-884564-48-8 $16.95 U.S.

35. THE SECRET LOTUS: Poetry of Enlightenment
Discover the mystical sentiment of the Kemetic teaching as expressed through the poetry of Sebai Muata Ashby. The teaching of spiritual awakening is uniquely experienced when the poetic sensibility is present. This first volume contains the poems written between 1996 and 2003. **1-884564--16 -X $16.99**

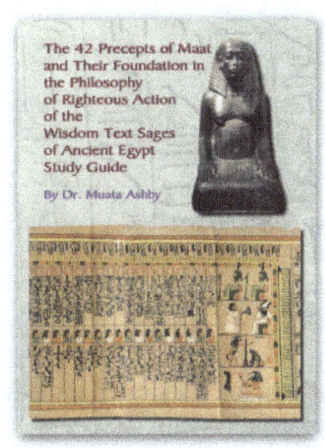

34. THE FORTY TWO PRECEPTS OF MAAT, THE PHILOSOPHY OF RIGHTEOUS ACTION AND THE ANCIENT EGYPTIAN WISDOM TEXTS ADVANCED STUDIES This manual is designed for use with the 1998 Maat Philosophy Class conducted by Dr. Muata Ashby. This is a detailed study of Maat Philosophy. It contains a compilation of the 42 laws or precepts of Maat and the corresponding principles which they represent along with the teachings of the ancient Egyptian Sages relating to each. Maat

36. The Ancient Egyptian Buddha: The Ancient Egyptian Origins of Buddhism

This book is a compilation of several sections of a larger work, a book by the name of African Origins of Civilization, Religion, Yoga Mysticism and Ethics Philosophy. It also contains some additional evidences not contained in the larger work that demonstrate the correlation between Ancient Egyptian Religion and Buddhism. This book is one of several compiled short volumes that has been compiled so as to facilitate access to specific subjects contained in the larger work which is over 680 pages long. These short and small volumes have been specifically designed to cover one subject in a brief and low cost format. This present volume, The Ancient Egyptian Buddha: The Ancient Egyptian Origins of Buddhism, formed one subject in the larger work; actually it was one chapter of the larger work. However, this volume has some new additional evidences and comparisons of Buddhist and Neterian (Ancient Egyptian) philosophies not previously discussed. It was felt that this subject needed to be discussed because even in the early 21st century, the idea persists that Buddhism originated only in India independently. Yet there is ample evidence from ancient writings and perhaps more importantly, iconographical evidences from the Ancient Egyptians and early Buddhists themselves that prove otherwise. This handy volume has been designed to be accessible to young adults and all others who would like to have an easy reference with documentation on this important subject. This is an important subject because the frame of reference with which we look at a culture depends strongly on our conceptions about its origins. in this case, if we look at the Buddhism as an Asiatic religion we would treat it and it's culture in one way. If we id as African [Ancient Egyptian] we not only would see it in a different light but we also must ascribe Africa with a glorious legacy that matches any other culture in human history and gave rise to one of the present day most important religious philosophies. We would also look at the culture and philosophies of the Ancient Egyptians as having African insights that offer us greater depth into the Buddhist philosophies. Those insights inform our knowledge about other African traditions and we can also begin to understand in a deeper way the effect of Ancient Egyptian culture on African culture and also on the Asiatic as well. We would also be able to discover the glorious and wondrous teaching of mystical philosophy that Ancient Egyptian Shetaut Neter religion offers, that is as powerful as any other mystic system of spiritual philosophy in the world today. ISBN: 1-884564-61-5 $28.95

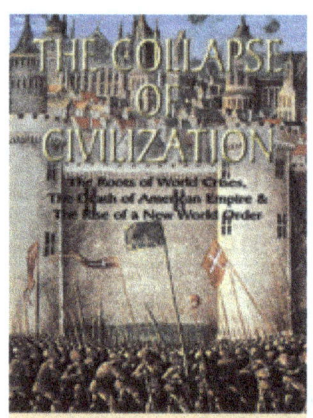

37. The Death of American Empire: Neo-conservatism, Theocracy, Economic Imperialism, Environmental Disaster and the Collapse of Civilization

This work is a collection of essays relating to social and economic, leadership, and ethics, ecological and religious issues that are facing the world today in order to understand the course of history that has led humanity to its present condition and then arrive at positive solutions that will lead to better outcomes for all humanity. It surveys the development and decline of major empires throughout history and focuses on the creation of American Empire along with the social, political and economic policies that led to the prominence of the United States of America as a Superpower including the rise of the political control of the neo-con political philosophy including militarism and the military industrial complex in American politics and the rise of the religious right into and American Theocracy movement. This volume details, through historical and current events, the psychology behind the dominance of western culture in world politics through the "Superpower Syndrome Mandatory Conflict Complex" that drives the Superpower culture to establish itself above all others and then act hubristically to dominate world culture through legitimate influences as well as coercion, media censorship and misinformation leading to international hegemony and world conflict. This volume also details the financial policies that gave rise to American prominence in the global economy, especially after World War II, and promoted American preeminence over the world economy through Globalization as well as the environmental policies, including the oil economy, that are promoting degradation of the world ecology and contribute to the decline of America as an Empire culture. This volume finally explores the factors pointing to the decline of the American Empire economy and imperial power and what to expect in the aftermath of American prominence and how to survive the decline while at the same time promoting policies and social-economic-religious-political changes that are needed in order to promote the emergence of a beneficial and sustainable culture. **$25.95soft** 1-884564-25-9, Hard Cover **$29.95** 1-884564-45-3

**38. The African Origins of Hatha Yoga:
And its Ancient Mystical Teaching**
The subject of this present volume, The Ancient Egyptian Origins of Yoga Postures, formed one subject in the larger works, African Origins of Civilization Religion, Yoga Mysticism and Ethics Philosophy and the Book Egypt and India is the section of the book African Origins of Civilization. Those works contain the collection of all correlations between Ancient Egypt and India. This volume also contains some additional information not contained in the previous work. It was felt that this subject needed to be discussed more directly, being treated in one volume, as opposed to being contained in the larger work along with other subjects, because even in the early 21st century, the idea persists that the Yoga and specifically, Yoga Postures, were invented and developed only in India. The Ancient Egyptians were peoples originally from Africa who were, in ancient times, colonists in India. Therefore it is no surprise that many Indian traditions including religious and Yogic, would be found earlier in Ancient Egypt. Yet there is ample evidence from ancient writings and perhaps more importantly, iconographical evidences from the Ancient Egyptians themselves and the Indians themselves that prove the connection between Ancient Egypt and India as well as the existence of a discipline of Yoga Postures in Ancient Egypt long before its practice in India. This handy volume has been designed to be accessible to young adults and all others who would like to have an easy reference with documentation on this important subject. This is an important subject because the frame of reference with which we look at a culture depends strongly on our conceptions about its origins. In this case, if we look at the Ancient Egyptians as Asiatic peoples we would treat them and their culture in one way. If we see them as Africans we not only see them in a different light but we also must ascribe Africa with a glorious legacy that matches any other culture in human history. We would also look at the culture and philosophies of the Ancient Egyptians as having African insights instead of Asiatic ones. Those insights inform our knowledge bout other African traditions and we can also begin to understand in a deeper way the effect of Ancient Egyptian culture on African culture and also on the Asiatic as well. When we discover the deeper and more ancient practice of the postures system in Ancient Egypt that was called "Hatha Yoga" in India, we are able to find a new and expanded understanding of the practice that constitutes a discipline of spiritual practice that informs and revitalizes the Indian

practices as well as all spiritual disciplines. $19.99 ISBN 1-884564-60-7

39. The Black Ancient Egyptians

This present volume, The Black Ancient Egyptians: The Black African Ancestry of the Ancient Egyptians, formed one subject in the larger work: The African Origins of Civilization, Religion, Yoga Mysticism and Ethics Philosophy. It was felt that this subject needed to be discussed because even in the early 21st century, the idea persists that the Ancient Egyptians were peoples originally from Asia Minor who came into North-East Africa. Yet there is ample evidence from ancient writings and perhaps more importantly, iconographical evidences from the Ancient Egyptians themselves that proves otherwise. This handy volume has been designed to be accessible to young adults and all others who would like to have an easy reference with documentation on this important subject. This is an important subject because the frame of reference with which we look at a culture depends strongly on our conceptions about its origins. in this case, if we look at the Ancient Egyptians as Asiatic peoples we would treat them and their culture in one way. If we see them as Africans we not only see them in a different light but we also must ascribe Africa with a glorious legacy that matches any other culture in human history. We would also look at the culture and philosophies of the Ancient Egyptians as having African insights instead of Asiatic ones. Those insights inform our knowledge bout other African traditions and we can also begin to understand in a deeper way the effect of Ancient Egyptian culture on African culture and also on the Asiatic as well. ISBN 1-884564-21-6 $19.99

40. The Limits of Faith: The Failure of Faith-based Religions and the Solution to the Meaning of Life

Is faith belief in something without proof? And if so is there never to be any proof or discovery? If so what is the need of intellect? If faith is trust in something that is real is that reality historical, literal or metaphorical or philosophical? If knowledge is an essential element in faith why should there by so much emphasis on believing and not on understanding in the modern practice of religion? This volume is a compilation of essays related to the nature of religious faith in the context of its inception in human history as well as its meaning for religious practice and relations between religions in modern times. Faith has come to be regarded as a virtuous goal in life. However, many people have asked how can it be that an endeavor that is supposed to be dedicated to spiritual upliftment has led to more conflict in human history than any other social factor? ISBN 1884564631 SOFT COVER - $19.99, ISBN 1884564623 HARD COVER - $28.95

41. Redemption of The Criminal Heart Through Kemetic Spirituality and Maat Philosophy

Special book dedicated to inmates, their families and members of the Law Enforcement community. ISBN: 1-884564-70-4

$5.00

religions and other aspects of human culture. It was originally introduced in the year 2002. This volume contains an expanded treatment as well as several refinements along with examples of the application of the method. the apparent. I hope you enjoy these art renditions as serene reflections of the mysteries of life. ISBN: 1-884564-72-0

Book price $21.95

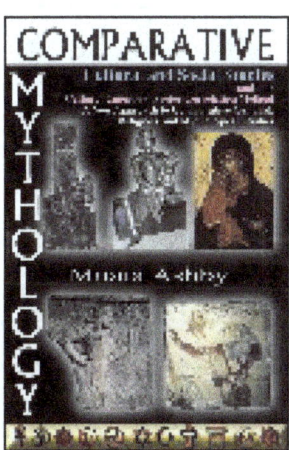

42. COMPARATIVE MYTHOLOGY

What are Myth and Culture and what is their importance for understanding the development of societies, human evolution and the search for meaning? What is the purpose of culture and how do cultures evolve? What are the elements of a culture and how can those elements be broken down and the constituent parts of a culture understood and compared? How do cultures interact? How does enculturation occur and how do people interact with other cultures? How do the processes of acculturation and cooptation occur and what does this mean for the development of a society? How can the study of myths and the elements of culture help in understanding the meaning of life and the means to promote understanding and peace in the world of human activity? This volume is the exposition of a method for studying and comparing cultures, myths and other social aspects of a society. It is an expansion on the Cultural Category Factor Correlation method for studying and comparing myths, cultures,

43. CONVERSATION WITH GOD: Revelations of the Important Questions of Life

$24.99 U.S.

This volume contains a grouping of some of the questions that have been submitted to Sebai Dr. Muata Ashby. They are efforts by many aspirants to better understand and practice the teachings of mystical spirituality. It is said that when sages are asked spiritual questions they are relaying the wisdom of God, the Goddess, the Higher Self, etc. There is a very special quality about the Q & A process that does not occur during a regular lecture session. Certain points come out that would not come out otherwise due to the nature of the process which ideally occurs after a lecture. Having been to a certain degree enlightened by a lecture certain new questions arise and the answers to these have the effect of elevating the teaching of the lecture to even higher levels. Therefore, enjoy these exchanges and may they lead you to enlightenment, peace

and prosperity. Available Late Summer 2007
ISBN: 1-884564-68-2

44. MYSTIC ART PAINTINGS

(with Full Color images) This book contains a collection of the small number of paintings that I have created over the years. Some were used as early book covers and others were done simply to express certain spiritual feelings; some were created for no purpose except to express the joy of color and the feeling of relaxed freedom. All are to elicit mystical awakening in the viewer. Writing a book on philosophy is like sculpture, the more the work is rewritten the reflections and ideas become honed and take form and become clearer and imbued with intellectual beauty. Mystic music is like meditation, a world of its own that exists about 1 inch above ground wherein the musician does not touch the ground. Mystic Graphic Art is meditation in form, color, image and reflected image which opens the door to the reality behind the apparent. I hope you enjoy these art renditions and my reflections on them as serene reflections of the mysteries of life, as visual renditions of the philosophy I have written about over the years. ISBN 1-884564-69-0 $19.95

45. ANCIENT EGYPTIAN HIEROGLYPHS FOR BEGINNERS

This brief guide was prepared for those inquiring about how to enter into Hieroglyphic studies on their own at home or in study groups. First of all you should know that there are a few institutions around the world which teach how to read the Hieroglyphic text but due to the nature of the study there are perhaps only a handful of people who can read fluently. It is possible for anyone with average intelligence to achieve a high level of proficiency in reading inscriptions on temples and artifacts; however, reading extensive texts is another issue entirely. However, this introduction will give you entry into those texts if assisted by dictionaries and other aids. Most Egyptologists have a basic knowledge and keep dictionaries and notes handy when it comes to dealing with more difficult texts. Medtu Neter or the Ancient Egyptian hieroglyphic language has been considered as a "Dead Language." However, dead languages have always been studied by individuals who for the most part have taught themselves through various means. This book will discuss those means and how to use them most efficiently. ISBN 1884564429 **$28.95**

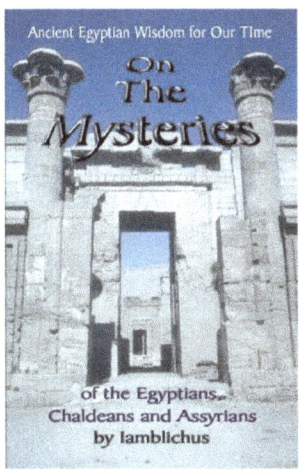

46. ON THE MYSTERIES: Wisdom of An Ancient Egyptian Sage -with Foreword by Muata Ashby

This volume, On the Mysteries, by Iamblichus (Abamun) is a unique form or scripture out of the Ancient Egyptian religious tradition. It is written in a form that is not usual or which is not usually found in the remnants of Ancient Egyptian scriptures. It is in the form of teacher and disciple, much like the Eastern scriptures such as Bhagavad Gita or the Upanishads. This form of writing may not have been necessary in Ancient times, because the format of teaching in Egypt was different prior to the conquest period by the Persians, Assyrians, Greeks and later the Romans. The question and answer format can be found but such extensive discourses and corrections of misunderstandings within the context of a teacher - disciple relationship is not usual. It therefore provides extensive insights into the times when it was written and the state of practice of Ancient Egyptian and other mystery religions. This has important implications for our times because we are today, as in the Greco-Roman period, also besieged with varied religions and new age philosophies as well as social strife and war. How can we understand our times and also make sense of the forest of spiritual traditions? How can we cut through the cacophony of religious fanaticism, and ignorance as well as misconceptions about the mysteries on the other in order to discover the true purpose of religion and the secret teachings that open up the mysteries of life and the way to enlightenment and immortality? This book, which comes to us from so long ago, offers us transcendental wisdom that applied to the world two thousand years ago as well as our world today. ISBN 1-884564-64-X $25.95

47. The Ancient Egyptian Wisdom Texts - Compiled by Muata Ashby

The Ancient Egyptian Wisdom Texts are a genre of writings from the ancient culture that have survived to the present and provide a vibrant record of the practice of spiritual evolution otherwise known as religion or yoga philosophy in Ancient Egypt. The principle focus of the Wisdom Texts is the cultivation of understanding, peace, harmony, selfless service, self-control, Inner fulfillment and spiritual realization. When these factors are cultivated in human life, the virtuous qualities in a human being begin to manifest and sinfulness, ignorance and negativity diminish until a person is able to enter into higher consciousness, the coveted goal of all civilizations. It is this virtuous mode of life which opens the door to self-discovery and spiritual enlightenment. Therefore, the Wisdom Texts are important scriptures on the subject of human nature, spiritual psychology and mystical philosophy. The teachings presented in the Wisdom Texts form the foundation of religion as well as the guidelines for conducting the affairs of every area of social interaction including commerce, education, the army, marriage, and especially the legal system. These texts were sources for the famous 42 Precepts of Maat of the Pert-m-Heru (Book of the Dead), essential regulations of good conduct to develop virtue and purity in order to attain higher consciousness and immortality after death. ISBN1-884564-65-8 $18.95

48. THE KEMETIC TREE OF LIFE

THE KEMETIC TREE OF LIFE: Newly Revealed Ancient Egyptian Cosmology and Metaphysics for Higher Consciousness The Tree of Life is a roadmap of a journey which explains how Creation came into being and how it will end. It also explains what Creation is composed of and also what human beings are and what they are composed of. It also explains the process of Creation, how Creation develops, as well as who created Creation and where that entity may be found. It also explains how a human being may discover that entity and in so doing also discover the secrets of Creation, the meaning of life and the means to break free from the pathetic condition of human limitation and mortality in order to discover the higher realms of being by discovering the principles, the levels of existence that are beyond the simple physical and material aspects of life. This book contains color plates **ISBN: 1-884564-74-7**
$27.95 U.S.

49-MATRIX OF AFRICAN PROVERBS: The Ethical and Spiritual Blueprint

This volume sets forth the fundamental principles of African ethics and their practical applications for use by individuals and organizations seeking to model their ethical policies using the Traditional African values and concepts of ethical human behavior for the proper sustenance and management of society. Furthermore, this book will provide guidance as to how the Traditional African Ethics may be viewed and applied, taking into consideration the technological and social advancements in the present. This volume also presents the principles of ethical culture, and references for each to specific injunctions from Traditional African Proverbial Wisdom Teachings. These teachings are compiled from varied Pre-colonial African societies including Yoruba, Ashanti, Kemet, Malawi, Nigeria, Ethiopia, Galla, Ghana and many more. ISBN 1-884564-77-1

50- Growing Beyond Hate: Keys to Freedom from Discord, Racism, Sexism, Political Conflict, Class Warfare, Violence, and How to Achieve Peace and Enlightenment---
INTRODUCTION: WHY DO WE HATE? Hatred is one of the fundamental motivating aspects of human life; the other is desire. Desire can be of a worldly nature or of a spiritual, elevating nature. Worldly desire and hatred are like two sides of the same coin in that human life is usually swaying from one to the other; but the question is why? And is there a way to satisfy the desiring or hating mind in such a way as to find peace in life? Why do human beings go to war? Why do human beings perpetrate violence against one another? And is there a way not just to understand the phenomena but to resolve the issues that plague humanity and could lead to a more harmonious society? Hatred is perhaps the greatest scourge of humanity in that it leads to misunderstanding, conflict and untold miseries of life and clashes between individuals, societies and nations. Therefore, the riddle of Hatred, that is, understanding the sources of it and how to confront, reduce and even eradicate it so as to bring forth the fulfillment in life and peace for society, should be a top priority for social scientists, spiritualists and philosophers. This book is written from the perspective of spiritual philosophy based on the mystical wisdom and sema or yoga philosophy of the Ancient Egyptians. This philosophy, originated and based in the wisdom of Shetaut Neter, the Egyptian Mysteries, and Maat, ethical way of life in society and in spirit, contains Sema-Yogic wisdom and understanding of life's predicaments that can allow a human being of any ethnic group to understand and overcome the causes of hatred, racism, sexism, violence and disharmony in life, that plague human society. ISBN: 1-884564-81-X

52. Guide to Creating a Kemetic Marriage Contract

This marital contract guide reflects actual Ancient Egyptian Principles for Kemetic Marriage as they are to be applied for our times. The marital contract allows people to have a framework with which to face the challenges of marital relations instead of relying on hopes or romantic dreams that everything will workout somehow; in other words, love is not all you need. The latter is not an evolved, mature way of handling one of the most important aspects of human life. Therefore, it behooves anyone who wishes to enter into a marriage to explore the issues, express their needs and seek to avoid costly mistakes, and resolve conflicts in the normal course of life or make sure that their rights and dignity will be protected if any eventuality should occur. Marital relations in Ancient Egypt were not like those in other countries of the time and not like those of present day countries. The extreme longevity of Ancient Egyptian society, founded in Maat philosophy, allowed the social development of marriage to evolve and progress to a high level of order and balance. Maat represents truth, righteous, justice and harmony in life. This meant that the marital partner's rights were to be protected with equal standing before the law. So there was no disparity between rights of men or rights of women. Therefore, anyone who wants to enter into a marriage based on Kemetic principles must first and foremost adhere to this standard…equality in the rights of men and women. This guide demonstrates procedures for following the Ancient Egyptian practice of formalizing marriage with a contract that spells out the important concerns of each partner in the marital relationship, based on Maatian principles [of righteous, truth, harmony and justice] so that the rights and needs of each partner may be protected within the marriage. It also allows the partners to think about issues that arise out of the marital relations so that they may have a foundation to fall back on in the event that those or other unforeseen issues arise and cause conflict in the relationship. By having a document of expressed concerns, needs and steps to be taken to address them, it is less likely that issues which affect the relationship in a negative way will arise, and when they do, they will be better handled, in a more balanced, just and amicable way.

EBOOK ISBN 978-1-937016-59-3, HARDCOPY BOOK ISBN: 1-884564-82-8

This Volume is a landmark study by a renouned mystic philosopher, Sebai Dr. Muata Ashby. It is study not just to philosophize but to be practiced for the purpose of attaining enlightenment. The book is divided into three sections. Part 1 INTRODUCTION presents a brief history of Hermeticism, its origins in the Ancient Egyptian Mysteries (Neterianism) the Kybalion and the origins of the personality known as Hermes Trismegistus. Part 2 presents the essential teachings of the Kybalion text, a set of MAXIMS, without interpretation. Part 3 presents glosses (commentary and explanation) on the essential teachings of the Kybalion based on the philosophy of the Ancient Egyptian Mysteries as determined by Sebai Dr. Muata Ashby based on studies and translations of original Ancient Egyptian Hieroglyphic texts; the source from which the Kybalion teaching is derived. The Glosses are an edited and expanded version of Lessons given by Sebai Dr. Muata Ashby in the form of lectures on the teachings of the Kybalion.

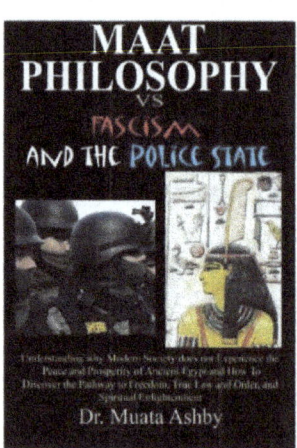

54-Maat Philosophy Versus Fascism and the Police State: Understanding why Modern Society does not Experience the Peace and Prosperity of Ancient Egypt … Law and Order, and Spiritual Enlightenment Paperback – January 1, 2014

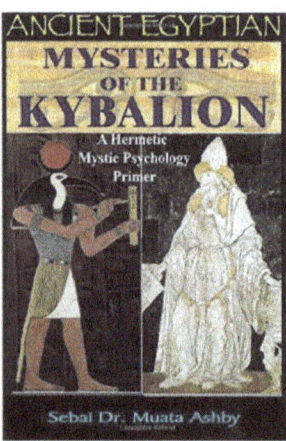

53-Ancient Egyptian Mysteries of The Kybalion: A Hermetic Mystic Psychology Primer Paperback – November 28, 2014

Understanding why Modern Society does not Experience the Peace and Prosperity of Ancient Egypt and How To Discover the Pathway to

Freedom, True Law and Order, and Spiritual Enlightenment. Understanding the Corporate State and How Maatian Philosophy can Leads to Freedom, Prosperity and Enlightenment

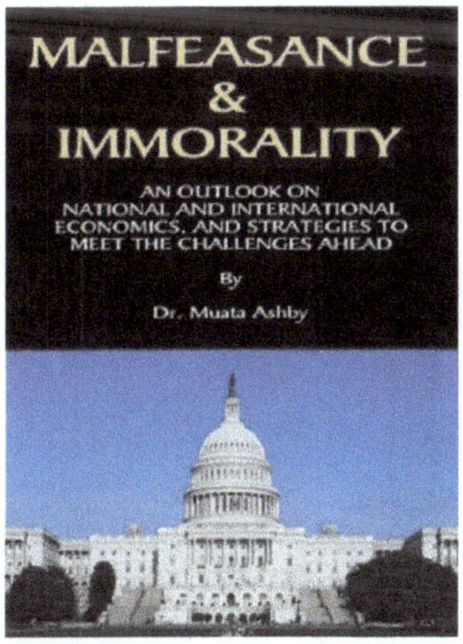

55- MALFEASANCE & IMMORALITY: An Analysis of the World Economic Crash of 2008, the Corrupt Political and Financial Institutions that Caused it and Strategies to Survive the Future Collapse of the Economy

The following is a first ever publication, by the Sema Institute, of a �White Paper�. The term is defined as: A white paper is an authoritative report or guide that often addresses issues and how to solve them. White papers are used to educate readers and help people make decisions. They are often used in politics and business. This paper serves as an update to the book Dollar Crisis: The Collapse of Society and Redemption Through Ancient Egyptian Fiscal & Monetary Policy (2008). That book was a continuation and expansion of issues presented in the book The Collapse of Civilization and the Death of American Empire (2006). Those books contained a detailed analysis of economic and political as well as social issues and how Maat Philosophy could offer insights into the nature of the problem, its sources and possible solutions as well as a means to develop an economic system (Fiscal and Monetary policies) that can work for all members of society. This paper contains an analysis of economic events and possible future outcomes based on those events as well as ideas individuals or groups may use in order to develop plans of action to deal with the possible detrimental events that may occur in the near and intermediate future. It serves as an update to the previous publications. This paper is divided into two parts. The first section is a summary which contains the conclusions of each section of Part 2. This was done so that the reader may have a quick and easy understanding of what is happening with the economy and finally, the actions that should be considered to meet the challenges ahead

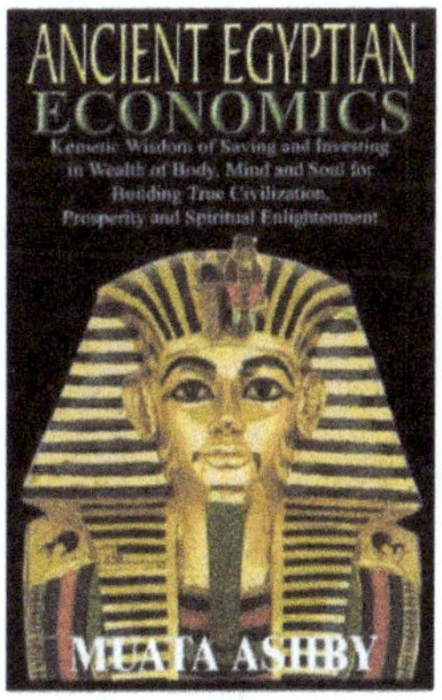

56- ANCIENT EGYPTIAN ECONOMICS

Ancient Egyptian Economics: Kemetic Wisdom of Saving and Investing in Wealth of Body, Mind and Soul for Building True Civilization, Prosperity and Spiritual Enlightenment------ Question: Why has the subject of finances and economics become important, I thought the spiritual teachings and Ancient Egyptian Philosophy and money were separate? Answer: Finances and money are an integral part of Ancient Egyptian culture as an instrument for promoting Maat ethics in the form of the well-being of the 'hekat'. The hekat are the people and the "Heka" is the Pharaoh. The Pharaoh was like a shepherd leading a flock and moneys were controlled righteously to promote the welfare of the people. In that tradition we have applied the philosophy of maatian economics to promote the well-being of those who are following this path as well as those who may read the books so they may avoid financial trouble as much as possible and have better capacity to practice the teachings. In order to have a successful life, human beings need a certain amount of money and wealth, but money and wealth are not the goal. They are a foundation that enables the true goal of life, enlightenment, to be realized. Therefore, we are only fulfilling the duty of transmitting wisdom about wealth to promote Maat, righteousness, truth and well-being, for all. This volume explores the mysteries of wealth based on the teachings of the sages of Ancient Egypt and the means to promote prosperity that allows a person to create the conditions for discovering inner peace and spiritual enlightenment. HTP-Peace

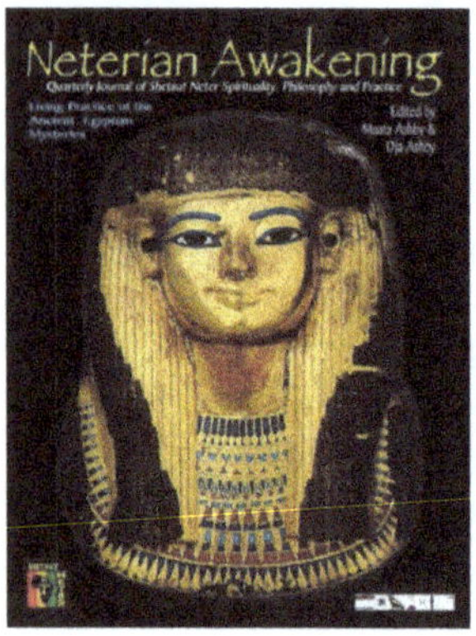

57- NETERIAN AWAKENING Journal of Neterian Culture Vol 1-12 In one Volume

This is a single file containing 12 volumes of The Neterian Awakening Journal. The Neterian Awakening Journal was a publication where the culture and community of Shetaut Neter spirituality was explored. In it Sebai Dr. Muata Ashby and Dr. Dja Ashby along with members of the Temple of Shetaut Neter presented articles, festival reviews, Questions and Answer columns and many other important aspects of Neterian culture and spirituality beyond those presented in other volumes of the book series that are useful in understanding the practice of Neterian Spirituality and the path to achieving a �Neterian Spiritual Awakening.� Part of its mission was: To promote the study of Shetaut Neter (Neterianism, Neterian Religion) as a spiritual path. Instruct the serious followers of Shetaut Neter spirituality who would like to receive literature in between the publication of major books that will fill the needs of their daily spiritual practice. Neterian Awakening Journal explores the varied aspects of Shetaut Neter spirituality not covered in the books. NAJ provides a forum for the development of a Neterian Community of those who wish to follow the Neterian Spiritual Path of African Religious Culture

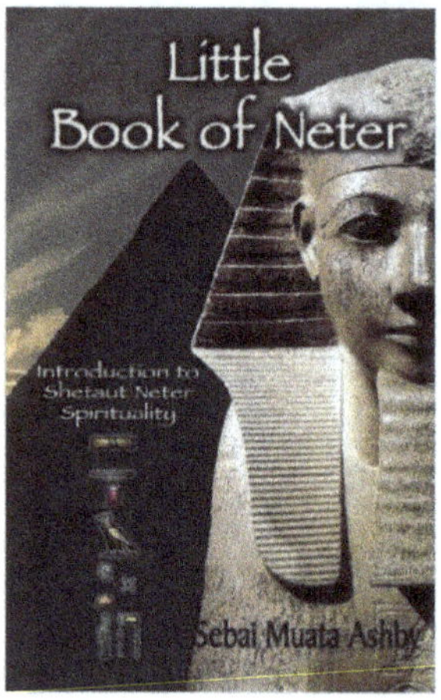

58- Little Book of Neter: Introduction to Shetaut Neter Spirituality and Religion Paperback – June 7, 2007

The Little Book of Neter is a summary of the most important teachings of Shetaut Neter for all aspirants to have for easy reference and distribution. It is designed to be portable and low cost so that all can have the main teachings of Shetaut Neter at easy access for personal use and also for sharing with others the basic tenets of Neterian spirituality.

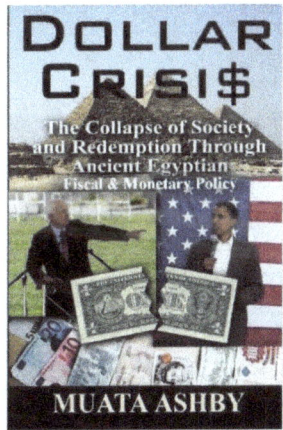

59- Dollar Crisis: The Collapse of Society and Redemption Through Ancient Egyptian Monetary Policy by Muata Ashby (2008-07-24)

This book is about the problems of the US economy and the imminent collapse of the U.S. Dollar and its dire consequences for the US economy and the world. It is also about the corruption in government, economics and social order that led to this point. Also it is about survival, how to make it through this perhaps most trying period in the history of the United States. Also it is about the ancient wisdom of life that allowed an ancient civilization to grow beyond the destructive corruptions of ignorance and power so that the people of today may gain insight into the nature of their condition, how they got there and what needs to be done in order to salvage what is left and rebuild a society that is sustainable, beneficial and an example for all humanity.

60- Devotional Worship Book of Shetaut Neter: Medu Neter song, chant and hymn book for daily practice [Paperback] [2007] (Author) Muata Ashby Paperback – 2007

Ushet Hekau Shedi Sema Tawi Uashu or Ushet means "to worship the Divine," "to propitiate the Divine." Ushet is of two types, external and internal. When you go to pilgrimage centers, temples, spiritual gatherings, etc., you are practicing external worship or spiritual practice. When you go into your private meditation room on your own and your utter words of power, prayers and meditation you are practicing internal worship or spiritual practice. Ushet needs to be understood as a process of not only an outer show of spiritual practice, but it is also a process of developing love for the Divine. Therefore, Ushet really signifies a development in Devotion towards the Divine. This practice is also known as sma uash or Yoga of Devotion. Ushet is the process of discovering the Divine and allowing your heart to flow towards the Divine. This program of life allows a spiritual aspirant to develop inner peace, contentment and universal love, and these qualities lead to spiritual enlightenment or union with the Divine. It is recommended that you see the book "The Path of Divine Love" by Dr. Muata Ashby. This volume will give details into this form of Sema or Yoga.

61- Initiation Into Egyptian Yoga and Neterian Religion Workbook for Beginning and Advancing Aspirants

What is Initiation? The great personalities of the past known to the world as Isis, Hathor, Jesus, Buddha and many other great Sages and Saints were initiated into their spiritual path but how did initiation help them and what were they specifically initiated into? This volume is a template for such lofty studies, a guidebook and blueprint for aspirants who want to understand what the path is all about, its requirements and goals, as they work with a qualified spiritual guide as they tread the path of Kemetic Spirituality and Yoga disciplines. This workbook helps by presenting the fundamental teachings of Egyptian Yoga and Neterian Spirituality with questions and exercises to help the aspirant gain a foundation for more advanced studies and practices

www.ingramcontent.com/pod-product-compliance
Lightning Source LLC
Chambersburg PA
CBHW081111080526
44587CB00021B/3550